HOW TO STEP INTO ANOTHER WORLD, DISCOVER NEW IDEAS, AND MAKE YOUR BUSINESS THRIVE

EYEBALLS OUT

DONNA STURGESS

I&D PUBLISHING

Published by I & D Publishing
New York, NY

Copyright ©2011 Donna Sturgess

All rights reserved.

No part of this book may be reproduced, stored in a retrieval system, or transmitted by any means, electronic, mechanical, photocopying, recording, or otherwise, without written permission from the publisher.

Distributed by Greenleaf Book Group LLC

For ordering information or special discounts for bulk purchases, please contact Greenleaf Book Group LLC at PO Box 91869, Austin, TX 78709, 512.891.6100.

Design and composition by Greenleaf Book Group LLC and Bumpy Design
Cover design by Greenleaf Book Group LLC
Photo on p. 51 by David Wilke

Publisher's Cataloging-In-Publication Data

(Prepared by The Donohue Group, Inc.)

Sturgess, Donna.

   Eyeballs out : how to step into another world, discover ideas, and make your business thrive / Donna Sturgess. -- 1st ed.

   p. ; cm.

   Includes index.

   ISBN: 978-0-9845859-0-8

   1. Success in business. 2. Creative ability in business. 3. Corporate culture. 4. Employee motivation. I. Title.

HF5386.S78 2010

650.1   2010930352

Part of the Tree Neutral™ program, which offsets the number of trees consumed in the production and printing of this book by taking proactive steps, such as planting trees in direct proportion to the number of trees used: www.treeneutral.com

Printed in the United States of America on acid-free paper

10 11 12 13 14 15   10 9 8 7 6 5 4 3 2 1

First Edition

CONTENTS

INTRODUCTION 1

ONE
Thrill!—Harnessing the Principles of Thrill in the Workplace 9

TWO
Live Action—The New Business Game 23

THREE
Sacrifice—Leveraging Pride and Sacrifice to Drive the
Social Agenda of Business Sustainability 31

FOUR
Faith at Work—Advancing Cultural Agendas
Around Inclusion and Diversity 41

FIVE
Recognition—Building a Competent Workforce 49

SIX
Badge Power—The Power of Purpose and Meaning 59

SEVEN
Happy Moments—Emotional Medicine to Increase
the Bonds Between People and Teams 69

EIGHT
Anticipating Action—Putting More Minutes on the Competitive Game Clock 75

NINE
The Business Game—Managing Strategy as a Real-time Sport 85

TEN
Dark and Light—Immersive Experiences as a Source of New Ideas 93

ELEVEN
Affecting Decisions—The Deeper Reasons for Our Choices 105

TWELVE
Standard of Excellence—Renewing Excellence 113

THIRTEEN
Military Might—Why the Military is a Talent Pool for Business 123

FOURTEEN
Top Ten Takeaways—A Call to Action for the Reader 133

FIFTEEN
Are You Ready to Take an Immersion? 137

SIXTEEN
Using the Immersion Experience 147

SPECIAL THANKS 162

Any man who may be asked . . . what he did to make his life worthwhile, I think, can respond with a good deal of pride and satisfaction, "I served in the United States Navy."

—PRESIDENT JOHN F. KENNEDY, August 1, 1963

INTRODUCTION

They are few and far between, and sometimes the wait for that flash of inspiration can seem interminable, but when they come, they can change us forever.

I'm talking here about *spectacular moments*, those very special and unique experiences that can lift us into a new perspective. They might take our breath away. They might send our pulse racing. They might make our head spin. That's how our body tells us that we've stumbled on a truly amazing experience, one that can dramatically shake up our ideas and impressions about the world and leave us with a whole new set of insights, a whole new package of tools with which to achieve our goals and conceive of new ones. These "Aha!" moments not only reset what we know, they also unleash new energy—sometimes more new energy than we could ever have imagined.

As a veteran marketer from a large multinational corporation, I understand all too well that it takes many, many good ideas to drive a vibrant company and feed the volume of growth expected year after year after year. These demands have pushed me to look in some unusual places to continue to find new creative inspiration for fresh ideas and fresh approaches. Put simply: I never stop looking, and neither should you. If a new idea comes in during an elevator ride on a seemingly ordinary day, great. If it happens while walking the streets of New York City or Tokyo, so be it. I don't believe in placing limits on inspiration, either its timing or its extent.

The proof of that became vivid when I had the chance to visit a state-of-the-art U.S. aircraft carrier. What might seem like a non-business experience actually provided valuable fodder for gaining spectacular new insights into how business can triumph in the world of high-level marketing and commerce, which has never been more challenging.

I was astonished from the moment I stepped foot on the deck of the USS *John C. Stennis,* a supercarrier stretching more than a thousand feet long and swarming with more than five thousand officers and crew. This was truly a world unto itself, a smoothly operating complex of man and machine humming with an efficiency—and mastery!—that people in the business world seldom match. I paid close attention during my short stay on the majestic vessel, instantly aware that the different world of operation and performance had invaluable instruction to offer. During my trip I catalogued a series of spectacular moments that stimulated provocative ideas, such as harnessing thrill in the workplace and building a competency in anticipation. These exciting ideas are presented in the chapters that follow.

Some of the ideas are brand-new in the business realm, and others are improvements on themes braided together from elements of both the military and business. A description of life on the carrier unfolds throughout the chapters that follow to stimulate the reader's own thoughts and ideas, step by step. Reading this book will offer a whole range of incentives, some obvious, some more subtle, to stretch yourself into new experiences and immersions that will stimulate your own creativity and add value to your own work.

But *Eyeballs Out!* goes well beyond exploring the novel ideas coming alive in its chapters. It is about the enormous power of an immersive experience to stimulate ideas—a subject described in detail in chapter 10. An immersion is something you undergo. An immersion causes you to turn away from the partial-attention world of BlackBerry monitoring and multitasking to a full-attention world. It is about undergoing an experience, truly giving something up to live it fully because of the potential payoff of the new perspective, fresh knowledge, or practical wisdom you can obtain.

And there's even more to it than that. For in these experiences the extreme focus of your mental and physical energy magnifies small things that ordinarily would go unnoticed. The noisy environment is shut out, and the intensity of the immersion produces a dramatic view of the new. Your senses are fully engaged. It's completely different to be pushed harder than you've ever been pushed, right out of all familiarity with your surroundings and how you "should" feel and behave. You have to be curious enough and passionate enough and brave enough to make the time and effort to pursue big ideas.

In 1966 Stewart Brand famously asked the question "Why haven't we seen a photograph of the whole Earth yet?" Brand even printed up buttons raising the query, and people stopped and stared. "Good question," they said. "Why *haven't* we?" Brand was articulating a yearning for wonder, an itch for astonishment. Then the Apollo missions began to send back pictures, and in December

1972, the crew of the Apollo 17 mission snapped a photograph of the fully illuminated Earth as seen from space.

The spectacular photo, soon dubbed the "Blue Marble" shot, would go on to become one of the most reproduced images in human history, and for those of us who can remember seeing it for the first time, we are unlikely ever to forget the experience. This now iconic image of the Earth started with Brand's curiosity and gave us a dramatic new impression of our world and its place in the solar system and the universe. It was like seeing ourselves in a giant celestial mirror. Our view of ourselves as residents of Earth could never be the same. It was, in short, a spectacular moment offered from the immersion in space flight.

Today the world is moving ever faster. We understand this and constantly look for solutions to the problem of how to keep up. Too often this search itself only burns more time and energy as we vibrate in place. Too often it only exacerbates the problem. The shorter commercial shelf life of ideas puts even more pressure on leaders to improve continuously and undertake nothing less than repeatedly reinventing their business. What leaders need more of are fresh ideas from the outside world. They need more new perspectives from completely different environments than business, where the assumptions and approaches and even the language are usually all too familiar. They need to venture out into the thrillingly new and thrillingly different. They must dare to immerse themselves—truly and completely—in the potentially transformative experience. A list of these immersion opportunities, which you can and should consider for yourself, is outlined in chapter 15.

As a bonus to the reader, you will gain some insight into the armed forces. These young men and women comprise a high-caliber talent pool for business, a point that is explored at length in chapter 13. The fast-forward maturity and skills development they go through is a college of another kind. Anyone granted the privilege of gaining an understanding of the carrier experience—either directly or through the pages of this book—will emerge with a new understanding of what it means when a résumé lists military service.

My hope in writing this book is that anyone who wants to can understand how a personal immersion in an unfamiliar world can illuminate powerful ideas that might not be seen otherwise. That ambitious goal means that some will find *Eyeballs Out!* a mind-changing read. Most truly creative ideas arise through making connections that previously seemed unthinkable. That's the "Aha!" However, be forewarned: If your vantage point is limited to the immediate interactions of your company, the ideas presented in these pages may surprise you. They make shake you up. They may demand of you that you change and evolve. That might not be easy. But that's the point, isn't it?

CHAPTER ONE

THRILL!

HARNESSING THE PRINCIPLES OF THRILL IN THE WORKPLACE

For months I had been counting down the days until my trip out to a state-of-the-art aircraft carrier. By the time I arrived behind the gates of the Naval Air Station North Island facility in San Diego, California, and toured a few of the eighty-one buildings on the base along with our small group, the anticipation had become so pronounced that it felt like a physical pressure. I remember feeling almost light-headed as we walked through a hangar where planes were being refurbished and finally into an office to receive our safety briefing. Not until we were standing ready to scramble on board the plane that would fly us out to the carrier, throbbing with excitement, were we finally informed that our destination would be the USS *John C. Stennis*—a ninety-seven thousand-ton behemoth, more than one thousand feet long—which was then doing maneuvers in the Pacific Ocean off the coast of San Diego.

Now that we knew our exact destination, every gesture or movement took on added significance. An airman demonstrated the flight vest and its pouch, containing a light stick, a whistle, and a giant tea bag of yellow stain that would make a useful visual target in the water in the event that we ended up there. The cumulative effect of the safety briefing and the demonstration of the survival equipment was enough to make it so that we weren't just being encouraged to imagine something going wrong; our thoughts were being jerked forcibly toward that possibility, just in case.

Waiting on the airfield to board the C-2 aircraft—known as the COD, or carrier onboard delivery plane—the change in our perceptions was complete. Everything we ordinarily saw, smelled, and heard had changed. We were already in an unfamiliar land, or at least it felt that way.

We were given helmets with padded ear covers to filter out the roaring engines. Large plastic goggles covered the top halves of our faces. All the passenger seats in the C-2 face the rear of the plane, and we were strapped in across the lap and then buckled in with shoulder harnesses that were cinched up tight to eliminate any airspace between each of us and the seat; we would be glad for that, we were told, once it came time to experience the unique landing that would end the flight.

As we headed out over the Pacific, I could feel the bones in my skull lightly vibrating in time with the interior of the aircraft. In the cocoon of my helmet and goggles, I had almost a preternatural awareness of my surroundings in the plane. Amazing how a whiff of potential danger can sharpen the senses! The interior was all beige steel and rivets, with wires and electronics undisguised and fully on display. This was clearly no cushy commercial interior. The steel shell of the plane was minus any padding to absorb the noise, and we could hear the airman's instructions only when they were delivered over a microphone.

As the pilot aimed for the deck of the *Stennis*, the airman shouted, "Let's go, let's go, let's go!"

In our briefing the captain had described the landing as something that we would feel in our lungs. He was right about that! What started as a rumble in my chest at wheel contact built to a roar seconds later as the plane hooked the arresting cables, which expand across the deck like giant rubber bands, and quickly reached full tension. Amazingly, the plane came to a full stop within 350 feet of touchdown, within four seconds of making contact with the deck, and after those four incredibly intense seconds, the pressure bearing down on my bones suddenly lifted.

My first thought as I stepped out of the plane and onto the deck of the carrier, my legs feeling rubbery but otherwise fully functional, was that it looked somehow like a LEGOLAND battleship—a gray vessel with figures in bright red and bright yellow and bright green jerseys placed here and there on the dark surface in front of us. A gust of wind off the Pacific sent the acrid smell of jet fuel curling up into my nostrils and gave me a visceral reminder that this was not Playland. The colorful action figures were moving quickly, and planes started to roll alongside us to get into takeoff position.

PLANE HOOKING THE ARRESTING CABLE ON THE USS *JOHN C. STENNIS* AIRCRAFT CARRIER.

Our small group was full of grins as it dawned on us that we had successfully landed. Unable to shout to one another, we settled for waving our arms in the air and giving the thumbs-up sign. No Disney ride any of us had ever been on could compare to the sensation of risk and thrill coursing through our bodies.

We were greeted by Rear Admiral Mark Vance at a welcome reception, and everyone was still on a high from the sensation of landing. The admiral described the ship as acres of the most dangerous surface on Earth, and we all exchanged quick glances. Somehow this comment only added to the excitement of the experience that was unfolding. Our emotions were soaring. Science generally defines thrill as "exhilaration in response to novel stimuli or experiences." Dopamine is released in the brain, and the result is a feeling of euphoria. Our heads were juiced with dopamine as we stood in the admiral's lounge.

Marvin Zuckerman, author of *Behavioral Expressions and Biosocial Bases of Sensation Seeking* (Cambridge University Press, 1994), has studied the importance of both novel stimuli and risk. His theory explains that higher levels of novel stimuli bring a greater perception of risk from the unknown and that this results in a higher level of anxiety. When anxiety overwhelms our excitement or arousal during an experience, we withdraw in fear. The business world is familiar with how anxiety and fear can sabotage an opportunity. However, in a situation where excitement from the novel stimulus overtakes our anxiety and continues to build to a peak, the result is a burst of pleasure—or in other words, a thrill.

What we experienced on the deck of the *Stennis* in the moments after the landing was the delicious afterglow of pleasure from the dopamine doing laps in our brain. It felt great. This was only the first of many peaks built by the novelty, arousal, risk, and exhilaration that we would experience on our trip. No wonder thrill seekers become addicted to this spectacular sensation of "feeling alive."

SPECTACULAR POINT

The thrill of peak experiences can be used in the workplace to produce a great performance and overcome a risk-averse culture.

In his book *Just Enough Anxiety: The Hidden Driver of Business Success* (Portfolio Hardcover, 2008), Robert H. Rosen argues that anxiety is an untapped source of energy that can be harnessed to drive change. Anxiety—and its cousin, arousal—are produced in the brain's limbic system, where our emotions reside. Arousal is a healthy level of anxiety, and it can boost confidence and increase your energy to act.

High-performance athletes know how to use arousal to drive optimal performance. So how can we in business use arousal to help employees embrace risk and have peak experiences that result in a pleasurable burst of accomplishment? Instead of risk overwhelming arousal and producing fear, as mentioned above, arousal can be used to build excitement in a business just as we experienced it on the flight to the carrier. Here is a simplified sequence of five steps to create business thrills:

1. Novelty: A novel stimulus creates the arousal and excitement required to focus attention sharply and allow learning and growth to take place.
2. Anxiety: Emotions modulate between arousal and anxiety. Speed and team motion can lead to spikes of both arousal and anxiety through the dynamics of competition and turbulent market conditions. But arousal wins out as the team members learn to manage each part of the experience and their confidence builds.

3. Risk: As the experience unfolds, arousal and anxiety continue to increase in proportion to the challenge and risk. It's why we all love a challenge!
4. Exhilaration: Arousal builds to a peak when goals are reached and challenges are overcome. Dopamine rushes in, and the team feels a spectacular sensation of exhilaration from the accomplishment.
5. Reflection: Post-reflection on the peak performance produces a surprise in the participants. Performing beyond your own personal expectations is a powerful act of recalibration for personal and team growth.

Abraham Maslow, author of *Motivation and Personality* (Harper Collins, 3 Sub ed., 1987), was right about peak experiences generating personal growth.

A great deal has been written about the importance of creating a learning organization. In the context of peak experiences, a novel stimulus triggers the arousal and attention necessary to propel people into motion. When a company is unable to foster excitement and arousal to offset the fear of change, mandates from management will often intervene. By assuming responsibility for the risk, however, management changes the dynamic. As ownership decreases, so

THRILL!
the cycle of peak experience

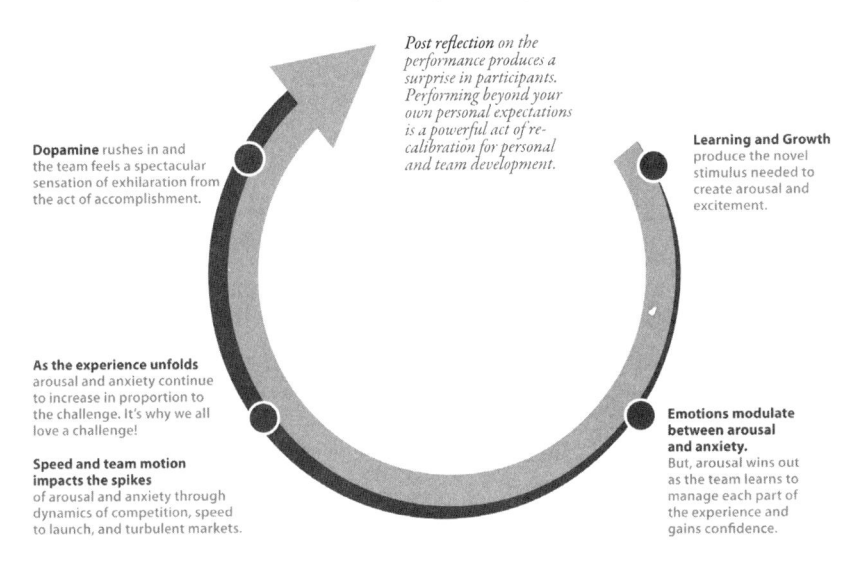

Dopamine rushes in and the team feels a spectacular sensation of exhilaration from the act of accomplishment.

Post reflection on the performance produces a surprise in participants. Performing beyond your own personal expectations is a powerful act of re-calibration for personal and team development.

Learning and Growth produce the novel stimulus needed to create arousal and excitement.

As the experience unfolds arousal and anxiety continue to increase in proportion to the challenge. It's why we all love a challenge!

Speed and team motion impacts the spikes of arousal and anxiety through dynamics of competition, speed to launch, and turbulent markets.

Emotions modulate between arousal and anxiety. But, arousal wins out as the team learns to manage each part of the experience and gains confidence.

does the power of a team, and vice versa—creating a vicious cycle. When the team is unable to own its decisions and to manage the building tension that modulates between risk and arousal, it cannot experience the thrill of performance. Yes, the work may get done, but the experience is changed; you no longer have an empowered team learning through the work, but a management-led team just

WHAT MANAGERS NEED TO DO

One of the primary responsibilities of leaders is to maintain the organizational characteristics that reward and encourage collective effort. Here are the supportive actions that managers must take to empower a team to create a thrilling performance.

- Novelty: Put people on a new and challenging project. Introduce novelty in terms of both the task itself and the unique combination of people assigned to it. Creating fresh teams to drive a project is an easy way to create novelty.

- Anxiety: Empower the group to modulate their arousal and anxiety by asking them to visibly monitor their own progress and make the adjustments necessary to meet both internal demands and competitive conditions.

- Risk: Senior management must provide some time to offer guidance and resources. Develop a risk map to manage expectations. Growth doesn't happen without risk, and those risks have to be managed with transparency to alleviate the personal stress for team members.

- Exhilaration: The time has come to test the performance. The pent-up energy from the team will burst forward as the project milestones and defined goals are reached. Wow!

- Reflection: This is the phase where workforce confidence is built. Team recognition and the celebration of results are important management activities to drive the recalibration of what the team members recognize they are capable of in the future. An effective evaluation procedure should be in place to pull out lessons and act upon those lessons on a consistent basis.

doing what needs to get done. These are two different experiences with very different emotional outcomes for the participants.

This leads to the question of whether thrill, arousal, pleasure, and exhilaration belong in business. Business is already familiar with some of the emotional counterparts, such as risk, anxiety, and fear. By looking through the lens of a thrilling experience that intertwines these positive and negative dimensions, we can more easily see the tension points of both balance and imbalance. Organizations want employees to be less risk averse. They need employees to be unafraid of the new experiences necessary to produce change.

To reach optimal performance, members of the workforce have to push beyond the point they think their capability reaches, just as the military does. Personal growth is tied to the discovery of new possibilities in others and in ourselves. As participants experience the "Wow!" from accomplishing more than they thought they could, this confidence fuels the continuous mental and physical demands that lead to repeatable peak performances.

Creating the sensation of thrill in the workplace is a super-magnet for wildly talented people. In the war for talent that so many companies are faced with, offering the opportunity to participate in peak experiences is a meaningful competitive advantage to snag talent. There is a reason talent is lined up at the door of companies like Pixar, Apple, Nike, Google, and Virgin. It is worth considering why, beyond trading time for money, people would want to work in your company. Organizations that facilitate peak experiences and unleash the talent they have will win in the end.

CHAPTER TWO

LIVE ACTION

THE NEW BUSINESS GAME

Once in a while the boat would rock. Nothing much, just a slight shift under foot, but enough to remind you that you were at sea. The *Stennis* is ninety-seven thousand tons of steel, and it cuts deeply through the formless water. The moon hung around all day in the far corner of the sky like a mascot of the sea tides. That first day was bright, and we headed out onto the deck to watch planes land and take off. The flat surface of the flight deck extends directly out above the Pacific's waters. No guardrails. No second chances.

The optics were almost dizzying, like looking out at an infinity swimming pool with a vanishing edge that made the deck look continuous with the surface of the water. During the safety briefing, we put on white vests with large rectangular holes cut into the back to serve as a handle to pull anyone back behind the red safety lines painted on the tarmac. Occasionally, someone's curiosity got the better of him, and he leaned too far forward—only to be unceremoniously yanked back by the vest. One of the crewmen told us they call the vest cutout the "holy-shit handle." No one wanted to ask about how often people actually ended up overboard—but we were curious about the planes. A large crane parked alongside the tower was pointed out to us in response to the question "How do you fish a plane out of the water?"

The deck of the ship is the length of three football fields placed end to end. But to a pilot coming in for a landing, it must appear as nothing more substantial than a small black speck bobbing in the ocean. The deck is 257 feet wide compared to the 160 feet of a football field. Now imagine planes parked on both sides and a corridor down the middle of the deck for landing and lifting off. We stood behind the red safety line, and yet we were closer to moving aircraft than I will ever be again. The golf cart–size fire truck stood to the left of us with sailors decked out in shiny silver suits, gloves, and boots. Beneath our feet were two nuclear reactors to power the ship, and its cargo included 3 million gallons of jet fuel. Up on deck, the combination of jet fuel, engine smoke, moving aircraft, and humans seemed even more dangerous and combustible. "Four and a half acres of the most dangerous surface on Earth," the admiral had said, and more than ever, we were sure he wasn't exaggerating.

The landings were particularly interesting to watch now that we had survived one of our own. The pilots are as skilled as artisans. Landing on the carrier is different every time and endlessly challenging. One minute these pilots are dancing with the clouds, and the next minute they are grooving with gravity to drop onto the carrier. Not all of the planes successfully catch the hook point. As they line up for a landing, the pilots accelerate the engines to prepare for takeoff in the event they miss the hook. The cacophony of roaring engines at full force snagged by the catch-hook cable can be felt on the surface of your skin. All ears on deck are covered in padded headgear for protection, which eliminates any talking. Hand signals communicate instead of words. Visually, it was an impressive production of colorful figures and assorted aircraft choreographed into synchronized movement with rhythms, harmonies, contrasts, progressions, and crescendos. Like costumes that define characters, the roles and responsibilities are designated by pants and jersey colors, a system that presents a stunning clarity of who does what on this fast-moving, highly charged stage of dramatic peak experiences.

SPECTACULAR POINT

Empowering the workforce is now the table stakes to play the faster ground game of business.

During a meeting on the Bridge with the ship's captain, Captain Joseph Kuzmick, he talked about his leadership style, using the word "empowerment" more than once. I told him about watching a fresh-faced sailor that afternoon in the maintenance shop rebuild a jet engine that would go back into the Boeing F/A-18 E/F Super Hornet parked on the hangar deck. The engine was completely disassembled, and it looked like a brainteaser game with the goal of putting it back together without any spare parts left lying around. I marveled at how much responsibility these older teens were given, and the captain replied: "Look, we have been doing this a long time. We know what it takes." That was the part I was interested in.

There are fifty-five hundred people on the *Stennis,* and the Navy sees potential in every young person on board. Two thousand are tied to air operations, and the remainder operate the ship. The activities we witnessed while on board indicate that the military has a higher expectation of young people than we do in the business world. In the business world, we are not so quick to empower twenty-year-olds with significant responsibility. To be fair, the power laws of the military are different from those in business. But what business can learn from the military is how to empower people for situational leadership and managing through risk. As mentioned earlier, empowerment is about giving people the power to act at their level of authority to make decisions and deliver accomplishments. It breeds the independence necessary to expand possibilities and gain competitive advantage.

Live action, whether in sports, emergency rooms, or the military, has to reckon with the clock. When action is occurring in live sequences, responses are the reactions primed by previous planning and training. There is no time to solicit approvals up the corporate hierarchy. If the world is becoming "flat," as *New York Times* columnist and best-selling author Thomas Friedman suggests, then businesses must also flatten out or else they will topple over. What is important about this change is that closer to the ground, the game is played at greater speed.

The master clock of the social-networked world runs faster. Business now has to respond in a constantly evolving context: Time to launch! Time to react to competitors! Time to reduce inventory! Time to adjust the price! Time to Twitter! Time to implement the next innovation! These responses—and many more—are now all elements of a faster, live-action marketplace.

"Empower your people" is the new mantra to deal with the speed of the ground game so that those closest to the action can operate with authority. Add to this high-speed game board the chutes and ladders of open innovation and open sourcing, and it might be a good idea to put the players in colored jerseys just to distinguish what team they are on and which position they are currently playing.

Perhaps it is quixotic to think we can come up with new methods to lead organizations in tough economic times, when having greater control feels like the right way to lead. In recent years we have seen bureaucratic business leaders who were unresponsive to market shifts drive their companies into the ground and scatter thousands of employees to the winds. The alternative is the flat, agile structure that interacts with open information and open sourcing, where power and expertise are moved fluidly throughout all levels of the company and beyond. The focus for management therefore has to shift from observing physical work in a hierarchy to regularly assessing achievement and results. Unencumbered by the organizational checkpoints, empowered people have the authority to make the right decisions at the right time. They are free to move faster than the company rhythm to beat the clock and competition. While many senior leaders agree that leadership has to be diffused through the whole organization, they find it difficult to let go and trust their employees. They must remember that one size does not fit all. Empowerment is progressive, and there have to be different levels of empowerment for different skill levels.

Since you cannot wave a magic wand and suddenly empower people, here are some simple steps to promote empowerment in the workplace:

1. Ensure that the whole operation has a deep understanding of the business strategy.
2. Clarify job roles with clear boundaries and performance expectations.
3. Commit to training—coach employees to take control and manage risks.
4. Empower people with the authority to get the job done.
5. Give support and encouragement as needed.
6. Request progress reports.
7. Praise and reward accomplishment and skill.

For the employees, empowerment is emotional, and it involves personal discretion and the freedom of choice to make the necessary decisions. A key component of empowerment is confidence: the motivation to pick up the mantle and act. Giving and receiving power is a two-way transaction. Empowerment awakens you to your responsibilities; it breeds entrepreneurship and has a positive effect on building self-confidence. Employee engagement is increased as individuals own both the problem and the solution.

Go back to the five steps to create thrill; empowerment has an impact on each phase of a peak experience by producing the positive energy to persevere and perform. High-caliber employees genuinely want to be empowered to perform, and in the fast-paced game of business, companies can't survive without those who take responsibility and are motivated by the action and thrill of delivering results.

CHAPTER THREE

SACRIFICE

LEVERAGING PRIDE AND SACRIFICE TO DRIVE THE
SOCIAL AGENDA OF BUSINESS SUSTAINABILITY

For all the jaw-dropping wonders I saw during my time on the *Stennis*, some of the moments that made the most lasting impressions came in the always-bustling ship cafeterias. Partly it was the energy and efficiency and scale on display there, making me feel as if I were on a starship cruiser out of a science fiction movie. I later found out that the kitchen prepares 16,600 meals *every day*. But as much as these visual impressions stayed with me, this was also the place where I was able to have conversations that gave me a deeper picture of life on board and how it offered lessons we can and must apply in business.

I was eager to hear the female perspective, and at breakfast one day I slid my tray up to a woman and asked about her experiences on the ship.

"Is it hard?" I asked her.

"You have to set your own boundaries in the work situation," she said. "Women may not be as physically strong as the men, but mentally we are equally strong." She fixed her gaze on me, flashing a confidence and an iron will that I immediately recognized. She explained that her team knew what she would tolerate and what she would not. I had the sudden realization that it could just as well have been me using these words while talking about my experiences in the business world.

For a brief moment it felt as if an electrical synapse had opened up and was firing between us. She searched my face to see if I could read between the lines and glean a deeper understanding of the toll that life on the ship had taken, the price that came with learning the lessons she had to learn. The corners of her mouth lifted into a slight smile when she saw that yes, I clearly did understand.

Her greatest struggle, she explained, is juggling her duties on the ship with the demands of being the mother of an eighteen-month-old daughter. Soon she will have to decide whether to stay in the Navy or go on to a nursing school where she has already been accepted. Her husband is also in the Navy, but not on the *Stennis*. While they are serving, their daughter stays with her in-laws. We talked about her immediate future, and she said that when the *Stennis* left for an eight-month tour that following January, she would deploy along with the rest of the crew.

I noticed as she talked about her nine years serving in the Navy that her face changed and her posture shifted. Her well-earned pride was shining through. I thanked her for sharing her story with me. Hearing the admiral's words echoing in my head, I told her we were proud of her dedication and service and grateful for her commitment. "You're welcome," she said as we parted.

Just to the right of the bustling cafeteria is the office of Master Chief Joseph Powers. As the command master chief, Powers is responsible for all the enlisted men and women on board, dealing with everything from discipline to promotion. He reports directly to the captain. Over his years of service, he has developed an almost uncanny ability to sense when a sailor is not emotionally in a good place. When this happens, he pulls that sailor off the cafeteria floor for a chat.

During our visit to his office, Master Chief Powers discussed the issues that we in business have in common with the military, such as talent development and retention. The Navy offers up to eighteen months of college courses on board as a way to keep sailors focused on their personal goals while serving. Clearly, the military has unique issues in dealing with such a young population;

the average age of a sailor on the *Stennis* is twenty years old. At its heart, the military is a people culture with the same challenges of recruiting and retaining the best people as in any business. But the personal dedication and commitment required are arguably beyond anything a business has to handle.

On the way out of the master chief's office after our talk, I found myself thinking again about the woman I'd talked to over breakfast. I shared her story with the petty officer walking with me, relating it to the master chief's comments on keeping sailors motivated and fully present in the job at hand. The petty officer stopped at the base of the stairs and paused before he spoke, looking deep into my eyes. He explained that he, too, had a one-year-old daughter at home. His wife was at home with her, but he was missing her terribly. "The Internet helps," he added uncertainly, clearly hoping that speaking the words could make them true.

SPECTACULAR POINT

Sacrifice and pride can be leveraged to advance the business agenda, particularly on topics such as social sustainability.

There are many motivations and forms of sacrifice, although it always involves a conscious act of transferring life or energy in one form or another. It is a contract of the heart. In his famous "I've Been to the Mountaintop" speech, Martin Luther King Jr. said, "When people get caught up with that which is right and they are willing to sacrifice for it, there is no stopping point short of victory." The military understands the importance of sacrifice. It realizes the extent to which the collective force of moral and mental energy is what sustains the sacrifice necessary in the preservation of freedom.

In the global arena, both the military and business, at their best, share a vision of making the world a better place. There is a cultural shift occurring within business that, from my perspective as an executive for a Fortune 500 company, I have watched unfold: Human values are more and more often entering the conversation. Business leaders are now turning their attention to global issues of social responsibility, such as sustainability, energy utilization, and climate change. Sacrifice and pride are important themes to leverage in order to tackle such large social agendas.

Lee Scott, when he was still chairman of Wal-Mart, went to Beijing to speak at a sustainability conference his company had sponsored, highlighting its commitment to offering lower-cost products that would enable people to live better lives. Addressing a crowd that included more than a thousand CEOs, Scott made clear that for Wal-Mart, the commitment to sustainability ran deep. "It is a mission people will be proud of for years to come," he said.

Sacrifice will be necessary for companies to transition from current methods and patterns of resource utilization to those with a lower impact on the planet. Multinational businesses form a suspension bridge across countries and governments; as such, they can play a role in organizing and driving the global agenda that has to be put in place. Individuals will also have to change their attitudes and sacrifice their habits of consumption to conserve precious resources.

Philosophers Henri Hubert and Marcel Mauss published prescient theories on sacrifice and gift exchange in *Sacrifice: Its Nature and Functions* (University of Chicago Midway Reprint, 1981), and these have useful lessons for us now. Hubert and Mauss maintained that for sacrifice to be justified on a collective level, two things are necessary:

1. Higher purpose: There must exist beyond the person something of greater value which causes him to go outside himself.

2. Relationship: The purpose must be relevant to the individual in a way that helps her obtain the strength, confidence, and benefits expected from the purpose or cause.

In order to shift the emphasis to social interests over private ones, sustainability efforts will have to elevate the status of participation. The status of achievement serves to counterbalance the personal or corporate sacrifice. To make the status of participation more visible, leaders can look to rituals and symbols from the military as well as religion for inspiration to make the status of participation visible. This is more than a question of simply making activities publicly transparent. Acquiring status symbols will elevate the importance of corporate and personal sacrifice and will generate the pride necessary to persist in the goals to save the planet.

Pride typically has more motivational power than money does. It is as useful to business as it is to the military in helping individuals persevere toward a goal in the face of personal sacrifice. Striving to achieve status and recognition can shape behavior. Lisa Williams and David DeSteno, in their article "Pride and Perseverance: The Motivational Role of Pride" (*Journal of Personality and Social*

Psychology vol. 94, no.6), conclude that pride serves as an incentive to persevere with a task despite initial setbacks. Pride stems from achievement, from mastering what one sets out to do. It produces feelings of confidence and fulfillment that motivate people to continue to perform. Dr. Jessica L. Tracy, in the University of British Columbia's Department of Psychology, conducted an in-depth study of pride and categorizes it as a "self-conscious emotion" that develops out of social interaction with others. Her work demonstrates that pride cuts across cultures.

Financial incentives or penalties have been proven to change social behavior, but only within limits. Wal-Mart's posture on the environment will bring some behavioral change on the part of its suppliers. The question is, what type of social system of recognition can be put in place to take performance to a much higher level? What are the "stripes" and "badges of honor" that can be earned by companies or employees to modify the conditions on Earth?

Programs that publicly award status for leading and performing will leverage pride as a motivator to accelerate performance toward sustainability targets. It bears repeating that pride has more motivational power than does money; it is one of the reasons people stay with an employer. Companies all over the world can instill this kind of pride in their people by linking to a cause for the greater good. Sacrifice and service bring individuals face-to-face with the hope and possibility of making a positive contribution to the world around us. Participating in social relationships and communities formed around this cause will satisfy both of the requirements described by Hubert and Mauss. These requirements should be a key component in building a system that rewards voluntary sacrifice with emblems of status that companies can be proud of. Over time, the status for social stewardship will build allegiances and become a bankable asset with customers and investors. In the words of Alfred Lord Tennyson, "Come, my friends,/'Tis not too late to seek a newer world."

CHAPTER FOUR

FAITH AT WORK

ADVANCING CULTURAL AGENDAS AROUND INCLUSION AND DIVERSITY

Chaplain Martie Johnson is a big, broad-shouldered man with a baritone voice and large hands, which he is never shy about raising to offer a gesture of comfort or support to the sagging posture of a visitor. Chaplain Johnson gets a lot of visitors. Everyone on board the aircraft carrier lives week in and week out with a background hum of inherent danger, and a steady stream of soul-searchers find their way to the chaplain's room. Chaplain Johnson sees spiritual health as an important element of well-being, and maintaining that spiritual health is both more important and more difficult when members of the armed forces are so far from home and family. No doubt he's right, just as spiritual health can often be an important but overlooked factor in the corporate environment, helping to determine whether members of your team thrive or falter in the workplace.

Going back at least as far as the time of George Washington, the American military has consistently provided for the practice of all religions. Simple common sense dictates that it is wise to keep servicemen and women of diverse religions fit and comfortable and ready to fight. In Chaplain Johnson's makeshift church of nondenominational stained glass, altar materials are stored in one cabinet and a Koran in another. Artifacts of numerous religions are stocked in the chapel. The chaplain pointed out to us the cross on his right shirt lapel and the Navy pin on his left lapel. Chaplains, uniquely, are an embodiment of both church and state.

Chaplain Johnson is a sympathetic man whose features readily slip into an open look of empathy and understanding as he speaks. In our talks he made a point of emphasizing that a sailor's family is always carried on board with him or her. They are in that sailor's duffel bag—and in his or her heart as well—in the form of pictures, stories, and purpose. As we sat listening to the chaplain tell us about these emotional ties, a wave of emotion washed over us. We could feel a palpable sense of the responsibility these sailors have to the people of the United States, as well as the courage and sacrifice of committing to a cause greater than themselves.

They herald a higher purpose of God and country, which raises the human spirit above the personal sacrifice and limitations of life on the ship. This is a source of great pride for the sailor, but one we visitors also shared as we sat there reflecting on the price they pay to do their part to maintain our freedom. It brought to mind a phrase from Homer's *Iliad*: "He serves me most who serves his country best."

SPECTACULAR POINT

Building a compassionate culture through chaplains or other spiritual advisors can create a better kind of business.

It's all a question of perspective. In the business world, we normally think in terms of capturing the hearts and minds of our employees. The military does not stop there. It thinks in terms of enlisting the loyalty and devotion of the entire person—body, mind, and soul. Business separates work life from home life. It compartmentalizes the two, as if each of us is two different people: work self and nonwork self. Managers tend to recoil or shrink back when issues and conversations cross the familiarly established work-life boundaries.

Yet for some companies, managing the whole person is seen as a way to build a more compassionate culture and a better kind of business. *The Economist* reports that there are more than four thousand chaplains tending to corporate flocks in the United States, and their numbers are growing: "Tyson Food ... employs 128 chaplains to minister to 85,000 employees [across its meat-processing business]." Many smaller employers also have chaplains, including Standard Corporation, Southeastern Freight Lines, and Dane Manufacturing.

As in the military, corporate chaplains care for all employees regardless of ethnic or faith background. This isn't just a loose goal. Chaplain organizations such as Corporate Chaplains of America and Marketplace Chaplains USA work to ensure that chaplains in the workplace adhere to the White House Guidelines for Religious Exercise and Religious Expression in the Federal Workplace. Different chaplains can take different approaches, of course. Some companies are expressing Christian values by employing chaplains, whereas others believe it is just good business. These companies have made cultural decisions about elevating care in the workplace. The chaplains are nonintrusive and available when employees want to interact. Their service is intended as a calming benefit against stress and even a strategy to minimize the capacity for workplace violence. Establishing a caring culture can help an employer boost productivity, morale, and employee retention.

Any improvement in the social and spiritual health of employees can be more of an asset than ever in the current climate. As Piero Ferrucci writes in his book *The Power of Kindness: The Unexpected Benefits of Leading a Compassionate Life* (Tarcher reprint edition, 2007), the trend in this age of rising globalization has been for human relations to become more problematic. Communications are more hurried and impersonal in our electronic world of partial attention, creating a kind of interpersonal Ice Age. "We are going through a period of global cooling," Ferrucci writes, explaining that the factors behind this shift include "new living conditions and forms of work, ... the decline of the extended family, the great migrations in which people are uprooted from their birthplace, the weakening of values, the fragmentation and superficiality of the contemporary world, [and] the accelerating pace of life."

If family affections, friendships, and human warmth are all on the decline, that means this is an opportunity. The workplace can offer a chance to reach out to employees to provide care services within arm's reach. Companies are quick to recognize the importance of both the mental and the physical health of their employees. But it may require a commitment to promoting social and spiritual health as well to being fully in touch with ideas of diversity in this global culture we live in—and to fully taking advantage of opportunities presented by the erosion of other institutions.

It is an unconventional idea to have an in-house chaplain in a major corporation. Then again, it is unconventional to have people do their laundry at work, the way they do at Google. That worked out pretty well for Google. Still, most companies prefer to keep the messiness of our personal lives pushed to the margins of after-work life. Many are fearful that having a chaplain makes some kind of overt religious statement. If a personal crisis comes crashing into the workplace, many companies offer employee-assistance programs contracted outside of the operation. External sourcing, it seems, has a different impact on the culture than do hands-on chaplain services within the company walls.

My prediction is that when a company begins to open its doors to participate in the pressing social issues of our world, it will start to humanize its corporate culture. Employing a nondenominational chaplain in a multicultural and spiritually diverse workplace can be a meaningful way to focus on care and respect and thus to advance cultural agendas in ways the human resources team is unable to. Through the resources identified above, the impact of a chaplain on inclusiveness and diversity initiatives can be easily piloted and assessed.

An alternative to establishing an in-house chaplain is to involve your organization in the Charter for Compassion. It is based on the core shared value of every world religion and moral code: the Golden Rule. Karen Armstrong's dream project, the charter was launched at the TEDGlobal conference in 2009 with the goal of leveraging the compassion inherent in all religions to unite people. Opportunities for companies to participate in integrating compassion into the workplace are available through www.charterforcompassion.org.

Here are some good reasons for you to consider integrating a care and compassion approach in your business. It can achieve the following:

- Cultivate a culture of informed empathy to effectively manage the interpersonal dynamics of difference in the workforce.

- Acquire accurate and respectful information about other traditions, religions, and cultures for employee training.

- Build a culturally savvy organization, capable of partnering with diverse organizations.

- Embrace the cultural contexts and difference of customers around the world.

CHAPTER FIVE

RECOGNITION

BUILDING A COMPETENT WORKFORCE

Even people uneasy with some aspects of what we ask our military to do for our country would have to agree that in the military, accomplishment is recognized and done so in a highly effective way. As in the Boy Scouts and Girl Scouts, there is not only a system of recognition in place, with badges and ranks and official commendations, but also an entire culture of singling out good work for praise and acknowledgment. The most obvious thing to say about this culture of positive reinforcement is that it works. We in business need to look for ways to emulate the military's focus on both negative motivation, such as that offered by the prospect of a reprimand or punishment, as well as the kind of positive motivation that also happens to feel good.

We're not just talking about "Job well done, sailor!" or "Looking sharp!" The sense of family on board is strong, and members of the family deserving of special recognition are sometimes singled out in highly imaginative ways. I remarked to one of our hosts on the ship that I was quite taken by the sight of a big brass bell in the anchor room. I was informed that whenever a *Stennis* crew member is married during a stop in port, his or her name is inscribed on the interior of the big brass bell. The same for any babies baptized on board. They literally fill the brass bell with holy water and baptize the baby inside it. That must make for some interesting photos.

SHIP'S BELL IN THE ANCHOR ROOM OF THE USS *STENNIS*.

COMMEMORATIVE INSCRIPTIONS ON
THE INSIDE OF THE SHIP'S BELL.

Why is it that inscribing our name on an object as grand and enduring as that brass bell gives us a feeling of pride and permanence and of being a part of something larger than ourselves? I don't know exactly, but I know the military understands why and understands how. The Navy is full of rituals like this that make people proud to be serving.

On our way to visit the munitions deck, we came upon the Starbucks counter located at the top of the stairs. Starbucks real estate on the ship? But of course! A stainless steel countertop was decorated with all the recognizable brand imagery, pump bottles of syrup, and paper cups and lids. The steamy sounds of a latte being prepared lifted an octave above the rushing air of the ship's circulation. Locating caffeine adjacent to the munitions cache was probably a good idea for any sailor not feeling at the peak of alertness while loading missiles onto the plane elevator. Several of us were ready to flip out our Navy cash cards and get our own latte or espresso or macchiato, but instead we were ushered past the counter to the steep set of stairs leading down to the Ordnance Room.

As I took the steps down to the next level, I could feel a pressure change against my eardrums and thought they might pop. This deck was below water. The sound of voices and the rolling wheels of weapons carts on the deck above became heavy and dull.

I landed at the bottom of the steel-lattice staircase, and my first thought was that the room looked like scenery straight out of the movies—not part of my reality. Rationally we all know defense is serious business, but emotionally you have to absorb it more slowly. My senses were on high alert with those weapons surrounding us in the Ordnance Room. The gun boss, a man in his forties, reassured us that no soldier had ever died during munitions training on his watch. My brain's alarm system, the amygdala, started to fire up anyway, and I physically recoiled from the large, spiky weapons arrayed before us. The men in our small group were fascinated by the power and engineering of the handheld weapons. But the sight of missiles and assorted guns racked across the floor before us took my breath away. I started to fidget.

A young woman, clad in the red shirt for ordnance personnel that we had seen up on deck, addressed our group and explained the variety of missiles. She was well informed but not polished in her delivery. She was probably the most junior member of the team, being given the leader's role for experience's sake. Others standing behind her were more senior and offered information only when she did not have the background for some of our queries and needed them to step in for her. Unsure of what we wanted to know, she easily rattled off the statistics of distance and impact. Her style warmed when we asked more personal questions about her training and experiences in munitions. At that point, one of the other officers stepped forward and proudly told us that she is very competent in her job. It was a declaration of confidence, a validation of her performance ability.

SPECTACULAR POINT

A public declaration of competence is a powerful motivator to build the confidence required for a great performance.

Sigmund Freud coined the term "golden seed" to describe a compliment or an expression of confidence as the greatest gift a teacher can give to a pupil at any age. He believed that when a compliment was given to a child in its formative years, that person would overcome self-doubt and be able to build confidence throughout life. For the Navy, such public expressions display a strong belief in the abilities of a trained sailor. They produce the confidence and nerve necessary for that sailor to perform under challenging circumstances. No doubt this is part of the Navy's formula for building leaders at every level, and it helps people to push beyond the boundaries of personal comfort to manage high risk. These declarations communicate to the sailors that they are valued and respected. They know, rather than guess, that their peers and superiors hold their talents and accomplishments in high esteem. This knowledge produces tremendous personal pride.

It's also a good way of communicating. As much as it's useful to have an apparatus in place for regular performance review, the simple fact is that a real-time assessment of someone's work will always have more power to communicate what you as a manager find to be good or valuable and what you find to be less so. These messages can often be conveyed through positive reinforcement at least as effectively as through criticism or reprimand. If a member of your team comes to meetings with a vacant look and seems reticent to speak up except when absolutely necessary, you as a manager could have a talk with that employee and try to give him a kick in the butt. That might prove to be effective. But another method would be to wait calmly and patiently for a meeting in which that team member speaks up more forcibly, and then to single out that team member for praise in the meeting. This kind of praise can be short and sweet. It does not have to strain for effect. Once again, if we go back to a basic understanding of brain chemistry, a well-timed compliment or expression of confidence activates brain circuitry that stimulates feelings of accomplishment and self-confidence. In short, one quick compliment in that setting, if given sincerely and clearly, can prove to be a more powerful force to encourage that team member to be more vocal and assertive in future meetings and discussions than a simple scolding ever could.

It is true now more than ever that leaders have to continuously recruit their best people and validate their contributions. Yet most cultures do not produce the type of validation that lets employees know how much they are valued. I recently received an industry award, and the first person to contact me was our chairman, who was on the other side of the world at the time. The e-mail simply said, "You make us proud!" I appreciated the comment. But my point here is that the military has woven this behavior into everyday life; it is not a part of awards events or annual reviews, but simply part of the culture. No one I know in business is told too often that they are valued. Giving people genuine validation (with an emphasis on "genuine") is an important way to deepen their connection to their colleagues and the enterprise.

The common form of a compliment in business is a "thank-you" for a job well done. We've all seen it a dozen times; it's a public pat on the back for your actions. Some managers are better at giving praise than others. A few like to deliver their praise in writing. What we experienced repeatedly among those on board the ship, from the bakers to the pilots, was a public expression of competence by a team member, a statement of skill at a high standard.

Try it out yourself. Tell a peer or team member in an everyday exchange that you think she is competent in her work. What is holding you back? No doubt it is that you work in a culture where such a remark is out of the ordinary. You wonder how it will be interpreted. That is the point.

Until people feel comfortable, it can be difficult. But you have to start somewhere. Don't make it a big production. Handle it in everyday language. Preface it with, "I read a book recently about how we should show that we value the people we work with." Or if you try it out with someone you know well, just do it as a part of the discussion on how work is going. Either way, the point I want to make here is this: Just do it. Just give it a try. When was the last time you rejected a compliment? When was the last time you heard *anyone* reject a compliment?

CHAPTER SIX

BADGE POWER

THE POWER OF PURPOSE AND MEANING

The sailors on the *Stennis* are inspired by a special symbol that carries with it great meaning: a flag found in the rubble of the World Trade Center. That flag proudly carried on board the supercarrier offers a material link to the most infamous attacks on the United States in our lifetimes or perhaps even in our entire history. It offers a powerful sense of connection to a large and complex story. The flag's torn condition and ripped edges bear witness to the horrors of September 11, 2001. It was flown briefly on the *Stennis* during one of the carrier's conflict missions after the attacks, but now it is mounted in the Stennis Room alongside a photo of some of the heroes of the New York Fire Department. John C. Stennis was a forty-year U.S. senator who stridently supported the military, and the Stennis Room was created as a memorial to honor the senator on board the ship. It houses his desk from the Senate and photos and memorabilia from his many years in office.

No sailor aboard the *Stennis* could miss the importance of symbols to staying true to one's purpose in the face of obstacles or setbacks. Each individual proudly carries on his or her uniform a badge showing that person's identity as a sailor serving on this awe-inspiring aircraft carrier. Even for someone like me, who had only a short stay on board, the sight of that badge still carries with it powerful associations and, yes, pride.

SPECTACULAR POINT

Creating a public badge system can inspire people to participate in a cause by making their dedication and sacrifice visible.

The power of a badge comes from its ability to unite people and influence behavior. A badge has social currency when it is highly visible and aligns people based on their collective concerns or interests. Badges produce pride by appealing to self-image or duty. In recent years we have seen the business world use cause-related marketing as a type of "badge" to attract customers and increase company value. It is a method for sellers to attract buyers

CHAPTER 6: BADGE POWER

THE USS *JOHN C. STENNIS* SEAL IMPLIES
PEACE THROUGH STRENGTH, A TERM COINED
BY PRESIDENT RONALD REAGAN WHEN HE
DESCRIBED SENATOR STENNIS AS AN "UNWAVERING
ADVOCATE OF PEACE THROUGH STRENGTH."

on the basis of values they share. Examples in the marketplace range from Starbucks supporting clean water to Wal-Mart promoting sustainability to Patagonia celebrating the environment to my own employer, GlaxoSmithKline, supporting HIV/AIDS relief and malaria control.

What social marketers and NGOs should do is develop a distinctive badge that is a physical icon of recognition for social deeds accomplished. In other words, the badges have to be earned; they are not bumper stickers. Otherwise, they would have no meaning. Badges have the potential to become beacons in the market that will enable customers to identify and reward socially active companies. This is a powerful way to have an impact on critical social problems while at the same time making a company's values and virtues visible to customers.

Remember the Good Housekeeping Seal (or, as it was known when the magazine first introduced it in 1909, the Good Housekeeping Seal of Approval)? It is still around, although it has obviously lost some of its cachet over the years. In its heyday, people looked to it and it alone for reassurance that vacuums and laundry appliances had a guarantee of refund if defective. Many organizations are invited to earn the Good Housekeeping Seal for their products and to display it proudly on the label as a symbol of trust and good reputation.

Similarly, if there were a universal Clean Water Badge that came to be well known and could have a strong influence on consumers' buying behavior, more companies would join Starbucks in supporting clean water initiatives. The badge idea requires that a company set standards or goals as a precondition for earning the right to display it. In the current business climate, companies need to build public trust in their organization, if not in their goods and services. Badges that can be earned for community or social support may be a useful vehicle.

There are two badge categories to consider that would motivate individuals and companies:

1. *Recognition badges* honor participation in a cause that requires a level of commitment and sacrifice. Recognition badges should be given for participating according to a set of standards. These standards could be based on time, money, or following required practices and behaviors. It is not enough just to mouth the words of support; they have to be put into visible action. Online gaming sites such as Foursquare, Bubble Town, and

Nethernet have good examples of recognition badges for participation. Badges with names such as Crowd Control, Fun Theory, Stop Motion, The Giver, Solar Catcher, and Weekend Warrior can stimulate the imagination for businesses looking to organize recognition badges.

2. *Achievement badges* stimulate skill building or significant progress toward a goal. Achievement badges should be of a higher status to reflect the greater effort or progress required to gain them. They must take into account what is believed to be a realistic goal and a realistic time frame within which to motivate participants. Achievement badges are the more common type of badge, and the best examples are in the military or scouting. Scouting badges are usually named according to general descriptions of the subject, such as Citizenship or First Aid or Swimming, and are based on rigorously defined criteria. Scouts also have badges of rank, however, as skills progress from Tenderfoot to Second Class to First Class and on to Eagle Scout.

Badges are a stimulus and an emotional trigger for others. The specific cause with which a company associates should be highly relevant to the customer and the business. Imagine if powerful, visible badges started to rearrange buying behavior. More and more companies would be looking to participate in social support that connects with their customers. These badges would ignite people with enthusiasm to join in the action. The more significant the badge, the more positive the emotions and subsequent actions it could generate. Participating in a cause generates excitement and activates feelings of confidence and vitality. These are the early steps of a peak experience and thrill, where the novel stimulus of earning a badge creates the arousal and excitement necessary to provoke new ways to advance a cause. In this way, badges can bring private and public interests together for the greater good. This may be particularly useful to companies looking to enhance customer trust at a time when public cynicism is running high.

Below are some illustrations that represent the badge idea. When criteria are established, they should vary for an individual contribution versus a group or company contribution. This is a new type of branding in the social space that can be used to enhance the existing brand equity value of any company or product.

Some may say it is too hard to set up or govern such a system.

Movement

Stop Waste

Eco Savings

Expert

EXAMPLES OF BADGES
FOR CAUSE-RELATED INITIATIVES.

Yet clearly the Good Housekeeping Seal was not complicated. The requirements were straightforward. Companies had to verify that they met the established standards. If the Boy Scouts and Girl Scouts can create criteria to earn a badge, surely the hurdle is not too high. Corporations with global scale, such as Wal-Mart and GE, could sponsor the start-up of such a program, provided it is not a corporate-owned initiative. It must be open to all who want to step forward to earn the right to wear, display, or publish their badges with pride. New networks will rise up to organize and support worthy causes when the sacrifice required is honored with a badge.

CHAPTER SEVEN

HAPPY MOMENTS

EMOTIONAL MEDICINE TO INCREASE THE BONDS BETWEEN PEOPLE AND TEAMS

I don't think I ever saw so many smiles on board the *Stennis* as I did the day we headed off after lunch to visit the ship's bakery, which has a truly prodigious output. "We bake 18,000 chocolate chip cookies a day," our escort informed us as we walked in our small column to the bakery. "The kitchen uses 30,000 eggs every day," he added. Thirty thousand eggs a day? That's 1,250 eggs every hour! More than twenty eggs every minute! About one egg every three seconds!

They gave us white paper baker's hats to put on before we stepped inside to meet the bakers and encountered a confectionary wonderland. We were introduced to two women making the delicious brownies and chocolate chip cookies we'd had at lunch the day before. The ladle they were using to scoop up the chocolate batter and spill it across the massive baking sheet was large enough to hold an infant. Around the room we saw all manner of polished stainless steel equipment used to automate the production of making many, many muffins, cookies, and cakes.

Yum! Sugar was spinning in the air. We watched as the cake decorator lowered a six-foot cake pan from the rack. The decorator had worked in a bakery even before he joined the Navy, but he gets more practice now than he ever did in his civilian days. Just that day, he had two six-foot birthday cakes to prepare. Each of them would be gone within forty minutes once they were set out; that's how enormous the scale of all food consumption on the ship is.

Not only were all of us smiling as we sampled the goodies, but so were our hosts. Everyone was in a good mood there among the cookies and brownies and enormous cakes. The bakers we talked to also seemed happy as they talked about their Navy service and the satisfaction and enjoyment it brought them. They like bringing happiness to everyone on board. Each chocolate chip cookie they bake and hand out is like a little bit of happiness freely distributed, and that makes them feel good. What the bakery really produces are little happy moments to make people feel a little better in the face of the constant daily pressure to perform at a high level.

SPECTACULAR POINT

Small moments of pleasure can be a meaningful disrupter of stress and anxiety.

The importance of those small moments on board got me to thinking. I realized that laughter in all its forms represents the business-world equivalent of a sailor on board the *Stennis* getting a smile out of a chocolate chip cookie. We all know this to be true, but in our focus on our daily To Do list and the pressures of an overcrowded workweek, we forget: A little bit of laughter can make all the difference in pushing back stress and anxiety.

Now, when we talk about "stress," we are used to talking about it as a negative thing, but there is such a thing as positive stress, too. Canadian endocrinologist Hans Selye, a trailblazing researcher in this area, coined the term "eustress" to refer to the kind of stress that produces positive emotions and good feelings. "Stress is the spice of life," Selye, the former director of the International Institute of Stress at the University of Montreal, famously declared. "People could live past one hundred by understanding and conquering stress, by taking it in our hands and examining its chemical and psychological properties."

Unlike emotions, which are centered in one section or another of the brain, your laugh track functions only when both sides of the brain are switched on. Laughter runs on a circuit that zips around the brain stem on a high-speed routing that cuts across several sections of the bumpy cerebral cortex. Laughter not only elevates our mood, it also contributes to psychological hardiness. People who laugh together are more comfortable together than those who don't, so laughter can literally help forge the bonds between people that strengthen a team and facilitate good teamwork in the workplace.

Because of its importance to our nervous system and its ability to handle and process stress, laughter can have a demonstrable effect on our ability to think clearly, particularly under the negative anxiety of time pressure. Recall the way that in peak experiences, a modulation occurs between excitement and anxiety. Laughter is a potentially powerful way to swing the internal pendulum toward excitement and to calm our anxious moments, substituting something much more fun and much more positive and constructive.

It's very important that business leaders have the courage to laugh from time to time, including sometimes at themselves, especially in times of uncertainty when a little laughter and fun is needed more than ever. We're not talking about a running stand-up routine. That gets old fast. But not every moment at work has to be serious and solemn. Laughter is a useful way to signal engagement with a group and can break the tension. It is a universal force that transcends language, culture, and geography.

In a study of NHL hockey players by Stuart Barbour and Terry Orlick, almost all of these premier athletes mentioned the importance of fun and enjoyment in their pursuit of excellence. One was quoted as saying: "As soon as you're not having fun, you are not going to play very long after that. It's just too hard on your mind." Several players commented on the link between having fun on the ice and their best performances.

Humor can be a powerful way for leaders to personally connect. At the same time, it sets a tone of taking a chance now and then and stretching a little beyond our comfort zone. A good joke almost always has an element of surprise to it. It shakes us up. The good, bubbly feeling we get when we laugh and have fun produces the optimism needed to seek opportunities and solutions—and to go on seeking them. So take it from me: Go on, laugh a little.

CHAPTER EIGHT

ANTICIPATING ACTION

PUTTING MORE MINUTES ON THE COMPETITIVE GAME CLOCK

Only twelve people have visited the moon since the first Apollo landing forty years ago. Their view of our world is something the rest of us only dream about when we tilt our faces skyward. One of those Apollo astronauts is Captain Alan Bean, a Navy fighter pilot turned spaceman. Traveling 240,000 miles from Earth in a fragile vehicle in 1969, he became the fourth man to step onto the dusty surface of the moon.

Pilots have to meet specific educational and health criteria to be selected as astronauts. Beyond that, they must also demonstrate the ability to anticipate and respond to a wide variety of new challenges that uniquely confront these people whom I like to think of as "space sailors." These skills are taught through flight training and basic mission training to prepare the would-be astronauts to handle the unpredictable events that can and do occur. Astronauts must also have the ability to anticipate and react to situations that are tied to basic survival.

Bean was the lunar module pilot on Apollo 12. Thirty-six seconds after liftoff, the spacecraft was struck by lightning, causing a power surge. The instruments began to malfunction, and land communication dropped out. Bean's keen situational assessment enabled him to respond quickly to restore remote communication in order to salvage the mission and go on to successfully land on the moon. We can only imagine the feelings he experienced as he finally touched down on the moon, when by all accounts the mission should have been aborted.

Bean's travel gave him an extraordinary view through the window of the spacecraft as well as a panoramic window on the universe when he stood there in the Ocean of Storms on another world. He now translates what he saw and sensed through painting, a hobby he picked up to unwind between space missions. The accumulated experiences and perceptions Captain Bean acquired through the windows of space are conveyed to the rest of us through the color and emotion of his space art. It is a translation only he can produce, based on his knowledge of space travel and his talent to express it in acrylics. He sprinkles a touch of moon dust into every painting. At the age of seventy-seven, Alan Bean can still be found painting in his Houston studio, wearing a denim apron with an Apollo 12 badge sewn on it. His gallery of work is available online.

At lower altitude back on Earth, we caught up with Captain Kuzmick again on the Bridge Deck. He sat in his elevated chair, with a panoramic view of the flight deck and the sea beyond, to continuously fine-tune his perspective of this other world of military and combat. He was wearing a bright purple turtleneck with the insignia of the *Stennis* embroidered on the chest; his jersey color matched that of the fuel personnel. Later, when we met the executive officer, he was wearing the same turtleneck in yellow, marking him as an aircraft handling officer. We found out that they honor their teams by wearing their colors. Both men had graduated from the U.S. Naval Academy in Annapolis and were pilots themselves, which we learned was a requirement to become a carrier captain.

The *Stennis* is a city, an airport, and a nuclear power plant. It has the unique capability to circle the world without refueling. But first and foremost, it is an air defense weapon, and its leader at the helm must be knowledgeable in air defense. The Bridge is a busy place, with young men and women monitoring the technology and computer screens. Through the glass lenses of windows and computers, all conditions on and around the ship are monitored. This is the seat of leadership on board—the place where events are watched and anticipated, where actions and orders are decided. It was hard to imagine how the energy on this deck could get any more intense, even when the *Stennis* is engaged in battle.

From the captain's chair, which I tried out, one had a full view of the operations landscape from which to anticipate action—something leaders in business do not have from their office windows. Visuals increase our perception and our ability to process information in order to accurately judge rates of change. Anticipation is the skill of looking forward and correctly assessing what is going to happen next. What is relevant amidst the streaming information, and what is not? People who can anticipate well can respond early to a situation, as Alan Bean did on the Apollo, resulting in a time advantage to make the necessary plans and actions.

The defense business often requires operational decisions in the face of emotional and physical stress—fast judgment at the right time. Sailors may have to make independent decisions in the face of overwhelming action and input. They must wade through continuously streaming data on conditions and changes, a feat that requires experience and skill to separate critical information from the noise of noncritical information. Their battlefield is just as asymmetrical and irregular as any business market. Unlike in the business world, however, they may not be able to delay a decision until the next meeting.

SPECTACULAR POINT

Anticipation is the action that puts more time on the competitive clock to give your team the advantage.

Look closely at a business with good timing and you will find it is skilled at anticipation. The corporate muscles seem to act and respond in such a way as to produce maximum impact at just the right moment. This stems from anticipating early cues and acting on the information faster than others can. Companies that anticipate well and are nimble in their response gain more time to maneuver. This anticipation requires people with strong perceptual skills—people who have both a high-definition sensitivity to changing patterns in the operating environment and the leadership skills to act upon the emerging information.

Let's look at anticipation through a baseball analogy. When a baseball is thrown, the path is determined when it leaves the pitcher's hand. The batter can anticipate a number of things about the pitch, based on the early signals from the throw. Now imagine if, in addition to the pitcher, the first baseman, second baseman, and third baseman could all charge the plate, as they would on a sacrifice bunt, and could each have the option of being the one to deliver a pitch to the batter. (One at a time, of course!) The random origination of the pitch changes the available reaction time of the batter to read the cues and adjust his stance. He probably would start to focus on the body language of the potential pitchers to better anticipate what will happen next. Then comes the moment when the batter has to decide to swing at the ball or not.

This variation of the pitches and the reduced reaction time are a metaphor for what business now has to reckon with under a digital clock that runs 24/7. Competitive curveballs are coming across the strategic plate with greater randomness, affecting the batter's ability to predict reaction time. The active and iterative process of anticipation is a necessary competency in a game that is based on speed. Many companies use scenario planning as a mental exercise to lay out the possible situations and options, hoping to structure anticipation into their plans. But scenario planning is only a tool. The real answer in this fast and variable game of business is to rely on situational leadership. By keenly anticipating what is going to happen, business leaders can quickly adjust their stance, allowing the business to act and react in the moment faster than the competition can.

Developing a competency in anticipation requires people who are capable of accomplishing the task. You need individuals who have a "touch" for the environment or situation. After all, you cannot teach a cow to retrieve a stick. Anticipating what is going to happen requires "fingertip sensitivity" and strong intuitive skills. These are people who are experienced enough, mature enough, or sensitive enough to perceive the earliest signals of difference and shift in the market. They know where to focus their attention.

You may already have people in your organization with these skills of foresight. Start asking around to find out who seems to be inherently good at this. Don't worry about their job level or department—you are looking for talent. Hang out with these individuals and find out how they view the business environment. Ask them what they would change about the business if they could.

Once you find people with anticipation skills, here are some recommended next steps:

- Create an informal work team of "anticipators" that gathers quarterly for a summit on the state of the business so they can exchange ideas and offer perspectives for management. This effort to establish a team recognizes anticipation skills as a leadership quality and as something the business values and wants to cultivate.

- Embed anticipators into strategic planning groups to inject a balance between formal planning and situational assessments. This balance will help steer the business.

- Add an assessment of anticipation skills into talent reviews to identify people with the ability to foster the development of this leadership trait.

- Identify whether incoming hires have this ability by asking questions about how they see the marketplace changing and why.

- Develop an emerging pipeline to give anticipated opportunities visibility among employees and a place to reside in the organization.

Most companies use trend data as a form of business intelligence to anticipate opportunities and threats. Trends identify broad, emerging themes that may be relevant to your strategic plans and should be monitored. There are excellent services that provide emerging trend data and indexes that you (and your competitors) can buy to stay on top of global shifts in human behavior and buying habits. To remain competitive, you must be aware of these macro trends. But if the goal is to increase the time on the competitive clock, then you must honor those leaders who know the business, the customer, and the changing environment well enough to sift through the landscape and identify emerging changes that matter to your competitive strategy. Their fingertip sensitivity to what is changing is the difference between your business and competitors. These subtle changes should be watched and monitored to determine whether and when they warrant greater attention from the business.

If it becomes clear that the change has increased in relevance and importance, the next question is, when should you take action? Determining the timing for taking action is a critical decision. A company that can move beyond hesitation to make fast decisions will be more nimble than its competitors. To quote General George S. Patton, "A good plan ... executed now is better than a perfect plan executed next week."

When decisions have to be made before all evidence and data are available, leaders must rely on their knowledge and intuition to move ahead. Napoleon referred to intuitive decision making as *coup d'oeil*, or "strike of the eye." It is a flash of insight that comes when anticipating a situation that suddenly gives you the ability to intuitively make a tough decision around matters of life and death.

In chapter 2, empowerment is described as having the confidence and motivation to take action. Empowered individuals have to be willing not only to pick up the responsibility and act but also to act within a time frame that delivers advantage. This requires transcending the natural human tendency to hesitate in the face of a decision. In so many companies, the culture supports hesitation and turns away from an emerging opportunity, instead opting to do market research, to collect more data, and then to watch and wait. Often it is not even clear what they are waiting for. When this happens, the opportunity that had been spotted on the horizon before others saw it now seeps into mainstream knowledge, and the competitive advantage is timed out. It is worth noting that in a tight race to the finish line, both the runner and the horse stick their necks out.

CHAPTER NINE

THE BUSINESS GAME

MANAGING STRATEGY AS A REAL-TIME SPORT

Standing on the hangar deck at sea level, we could see celestial blue and aquatic blue touching to form a blue-green oneness. The Pacific Ocean is a big place, and the view from the large opening on the hangar deck went on and on and on. The supersized hole in the side of the deck opens the way for the freight elevator to lower planes down to the hangar for maintenance. Again and again, a deep *boom* rang through our ears as a plane landed on the deck above.

I don't know anybody who didn't dream of flying as a child; it is an important part of our dreams. Graham Hawkes had unusual dreams; his were dreams of flying underwater. Now recognized internationally as an ocean engineer and inventor, Hawkes has been responsible for the design of Deep Flight winged submersibles. The Deep Flight Super Falcon looks like an airplane and flies like an airplane, except it goes underwater to explore the deep sea. It uses the configuration of the U.S. Air Force A10 plane and the dynamic principles of a conventional airliner, complete with wings, a propeller, and a tail.

Earth is an ocean planet, but the oceans of the world remain one of the great mysteries to be explored. Only the U.S. Navy has been able devise a craft to make the lowest dive on record at the deepest part of the ocean, known as Challenger Deep, in the Mariana Trench off the island of Guam. At nearly 36,000 feet, this area of the ocean is 7,000 feet deeper than Mount Everest is high. The deep ocean is truly an alien world, populated with strange creatures and hidden secrets.

Leaving the underwater deck level, we marched back up several flights of steel staircases to the Island Tower. It rises three levels above the ship deck (yes, we were huffing and puffing by then), and the three decks in this section were the Captain's Bridge, the Flag Bridge, and the Pri-Fly (or Primary Flight) Deck. The Pri-Fly is where we found the air boss, Captain Gordon Smith, who controls all aircraft taking off, landing, and in flight within five nautical miles of the ship. This center determines when and where each aircraft is moved, stored, maintained, and fueled. Together the airmen track and record all aircraft launch and recovery information; they control everything from the radio equipment to the fire truck. During flight operations this is one of the busiest places on the carrier as they manage the high-risk situations we witnessed up on deck.

There was barely any room to move in the cramped quarters as a few of us squeezed in to watch the team in action. The small team of airmen we observed was handpicked from other air divisions to work the "Ouija board." It is a wooden replica of the deck, with toy planes and helicopters that represent the scene on the deck moment by moment. The airmen were crowded around this replica, continuously changing the positions of certain toy planes and removing others as they take off or go below deck for maintenance. It looked like a fast game of checkers as these toy aircraft pieces hopscotched across the board.

The Navy's so-called Ouija board is an effective tool to represent a rapidly changing deck scene while managing the high-risk situation of incoming planes and deck maneuvers. In business we use mental models to make sense of markets and their dynamics. Most strategic work to guide decisions involves the tools of the analyst, such as documents, spreadsheets, graphs, and grids. We put together such charts as a SWOT analysis to look at strengths, weaknesses, opportunities, and threats; a GAP analysis to look at what we might be missing; and so on. This assorted bundle of charts and statistics is pulled together to shape a strategic plan that will guide decisions throughout the operation.

In the high drama of business today, however, these carefully crafted strategic plans can become out-of-date not long after the ink has dried. It begs the question, "Shouldn't strategic plans be more dynamic and responsive, like the Ouija board?" Outsmarting competitors involves your actions and their counteractions. Yet traditional strategic planning relies on *assumptions* about competitors' future reactions. War gaming and scenario planning are better tools for forecasting positions and moves, but the output still ages quickly.

Let's consider what strategy work could look like if you took it to the next level of strategic gaming. Yes, I literally mean gaming. Gaming is not new to business. War gaming is an ancient art developed by the military and later adopted by business as a useful tool to envision competitive positions and possible responses. In the online world, game development has focused primarily on fantasy and entertainment. So why not create a market for business games: an X-biz-box? This idea is not to be confused with the genre of online business simulation games to teach business principles and economics. What I am suggesting is a real-world, real-time application of game technology to build and manage your business strategy.

SPECTACULAR POINT
Develop an X-box-type game to manage business strategy as a real-time sport.

In this climate of uncertainty, leaders must begin to embrace strategy as an interactive activity rather than an annual planning one. Perhaps the planning tools used today are simply too broad and conceptual to drive an empowered workforce. The economic crisis of 2008 and 2009 showed that many companies did a terrible job managing their business strategy and risk, posting billions of dollars of loss. Clearly, something is fundamentally wrong with the way strategy is managed in the business world. This is a wake-up call, telling us that a large scoop of reality must be mixed into the planning process. The architecture and visualization involved in gaming have the potential to outperform current methods by making strategic work less conceptual, simpler, and more interactive with real-time activity. Strategy could be managed *live* rather than remaining as a reference document that has been approved and passed around in a binder.

The concept is a bit like sailing. The changing directions of the winds force the sailor to tack to keep moving. Each change in direction is not wasted effort but a strategy in action, emerging from direct contact with the environment. It is a constant unfolding and enfolding of intent. In this way, the strategy of sailing, like the strategy of business, is a live interaction with the environmental conditions.

The nonprofit organization Games for Change is an example of using interactive games to explore live issues. The company's philosophy is to use the systems thinking of gaming to engage in social issues ranging from politics to human rights to economics to news. The Budget Hero game gives you a chance to play with the $3.7 trillion U.S. government budget, ten years out. It is updated to include the federal stimulus packages and bailouts from estimates out of the Congressional Budget Office. The game illustrates your budget choices and how the debt rises or falls based on decisions you make. A tab labeled "The Data" provides easy access to the source material and assumptions the game operates on. It is easy to see how this type of approach could be used as a simple blue-

The secret to discovery is to never believe existing facts.

—Bryant H. McGill

print to develop a strategy game for business to explore actions and implications.

In the future, companies will have to lean into opportunities with more aggressive approaches and adopt a more offensive strategy. Events that threaten a business exact a toll by draining energy even when the response is positive. Some people are risk takers, and others are risk avoiders. The same can be said of organizations. Those companies that do not learn to manage risk better than they do today will fail. We will live with volatility in our marketing and sales plans for some time to come, and we must adjust our operating methods to better navigate in these rough waters. Future battles will feel different and have a far less predictable financial outcome. Maintaining multiple sets of conditional sales projections and budgets only throws mud into the organization. A strategy game customized for your business could magnify the playing field where the strategic plan and market conditions interact, making it clean and clear for everyone in the company to see the evolving impact. The game could identify emerging risks and produce a time advantage for participants as they calculate optional moves to reduce risks and grab market share. It would also enable an empowered workforce to engage with strategy in real time to make optimal decisions. It might even be fun!

CHAPTER TEN

DARK AND LIGHT

IMMERSIVE EXPERIENCES
AS A SOURCE OF NEW IDEAS

At night the deck of an aircraft carrier is significantly more dangerous, so we were restricted to a viewing deck on the *Stennis*'s Island Tower to watch maneuvers and stare out at a band of hot pink air separating the water from the darkening evening sky. As I watched one night, the sun fell below the horizon and the pink ribbon slowly evaporated. Minus any overhead lights, the deck appeared before us in geometric shades of black and gray, with shadowy figures moving about. The pilots have only the Optical Landing System, also called "the meatball," to line up their aircraft with the light strips on deck. The amber donut of the meatball centered on the navigation system indicates when they are on speed. Green and red chevrons signal the need to speed up or to slow down. The landing signal officers we had seen during the day were not visible at night from our perch, but I trusted they were out there. Their job is to talk the pilots through the final landing approach.

It turned out to be a star-spangled night. The moonlight was bright against a navy blue sky, and a multitude of stars shimmered as silent witnesses to the air show. Against this beautiful backdrop, we watched the dramatic scenes involving the incoming aircraft. It is significantly more difficult to land at night, and pilots who missed the catch hook circled back and tried again. The bustle of aircraft on and off the deck is spectacular. The crew can launch two aircraft and land one every forty seconds in daylight (every minute at night). This is a stress test of performance of the highest order.

As the evening progressed, the deck continued to fill with helicopters and planes—Super Hornets, Prowlers, Blue Diamonds, and Seahawks—all coming back from flight operations to park for the night. The wings fold up vertically alongside the fuselage at the push of a button, as if the planes were origami steel birds, enabling them to sleep side by side along the edge of the deck. Their giant tails dangle out over the water, no doubt intimidating the nearby fish. The logistical nightmare of parking all the planes on board came down to a synchronized set of moves between the Pri-Fly deck and the yellow jerseys.

Life on the ship runs continuously. The hallways bustle at all hours with pilots, crew, and sailors, all walking with a purpose. At sundown the hall lighting switches from white to a deep red full of warmth and vitality. That was a better way to think of it than as the color of danger. In the red glow our vision was much more limited. Stepping through the raised doorway hatches and climbing stairs required a sense of touch and a good grip to make your way to the sleeping quarters. Tripping or falling would introduce soft flesh to hard steel.

As visiting "dignitaries," we had luxury accommodations on board. I slept in a two-person cabin with bunk beds. Compare this to the sailors' accommodations, with as many as eighty people in a room. According to the sergeant who shepherded us through part of one afternoon, he sleeps in a room with bunk beds stacked three high and a footlocker trio at the foot rail. My cabin mate Jeanne and I each had a desk that folded down. A TV was suspended from the ceiling above a sink. The space was cozy—close but comfortable. We were grateful to find a bathroom located next to our cabin. The labyrinth of featureless corridors that lead to twenty-five hundred compartments on board seemed daunting without a decoder ring for the reference numbers painted on the walls at intersecting hallways.

Our onboard sleeping quarters were a new theater of unfamiliar sounds, starting with rhythmic booms cascading downward as planes continued to land on the deck above us. I imagine it's a sound the sailors no longer notice. Around one o'clock in the morning, we discovered, the crew drags chains across the deck to lock down the forty planes for the night. Eventually the percussion trailed off, and the night threw open a window to the day's thoughts and ideas blooming in my mind. I was fully immersed in this experience in every way one could be. I was literally immersed below water in my sleeping chamber, and my mind was fully absorbed by the fragments of experience and pieces of information that were filing into my memory banks. Each fragment bumped up against what I knew and caffeinated my thoughts, making it hard to doze off.

SPECTACULAR POINT

Fully immersing yourself in an experience illuminates new ideas.

What keeps business leaders up at night are not the new ideas blooming, but the worries of delivering on growth projections and raising shareholder value. In tough economic times, business as usual will not do. Night maneuvers on the carrier are a great metaphor for the increased dangers that shifting economic conditions present to business. Like the plane searching for the deck on which to land in the dark, a business needs to search for places and spaces to touch down and create growth. An immersive experience may be one such place to land, look around, and find new opportunities.

An immersion is something you undergo. Immersions cause you to turn away from the partial-attention world to a full-attention world. Immersions are about undergoing an experience for the new perspective, knowledge, or practical wisdom that you can thereby obtain. But there's more, for in these experiences, the extreme focus of your mental and physical energy magnifies small things that normally go unnoticed. The noisy environment is shut out, and the intensity of the immersion produces a dramatic view of the new. Your senses are fully engaged. It is like the difference between standing in the ocean *looking down* at the surface of the water versus putting on a face mask and plunging your head *into* the water. At the surface, the glare and reflection off the water prevent you from seeing any deeper than the surface. You are unaware of what you are missing. Yet when you puncture the surface and go below, the noise and activity from above are immediately shut out. It opens up a whole new world.

As with any new adventure, you may not know what you will get out of an immersive experience. It starts with the mind-set of the adventurer, not the planner. You should expect to be stretched by the newness of the situation and experience.

Part of the value of an immersion is returning to the experience of being a beginner. When we learn something new, our thinking slows down and we absorb information differently. The brain has a relaxation response that allows for insight and the emergence of other options. New connections are made during this time because we are sifting and sorting information differently as a beginner than we do as a professional. Our whole body is involved in the experience—it is not just a mental exercise like the activities at work. The new stimulus bumps and rattles our operating assumptions as we seek to put the learning into a context; these new relationships start to rearrange our existing stores of information into novel patterns to produce new thoughts. This is where original ideas float free and opportunities are discovered. It doesn't have to be quick. The stimulus from the experience will continue to percolate in your subconscious after the event is over. One thing is certain: Afterward you will feel the shift, the impact of the immersion.

In his 1976 essay "Destruction and Creation," Colonel John R. Boyd saw the nature of creativity as the breaking down of elements, the shattering of the relationship between the parts and the whole. He called this "destructive deduction." The many assorted parts can be seen independently and then are available to synthesize together in new, creative ways. Boyd was a U.S. Air Force fighter pilot and a great strategic thinker. He thought about creative concepts and decision making as stemming from either analysis or synthesis. *Analysis* proceeds from the general to the specific, while the opposite happens in *synthesis,* which proceeds from the specific to the general. Said another way, analysis is deductive thinking and synthesis is inductive thinking.

An immersive experience offers a physical cinema of creative content for building ideas. Boyd saw the value of finding new pieces or fragments of ideas in order to create something new. Let's review the fragments of ideas that have contributed to the Spectacular Points of the first few chapters. The deconstructed parts are shown on the next page. Seen through the immersion, these ideas have been synthesized into something new.

If analysis is deductive thinking and synthesis is inductive thinking, in an immersion, conductive thinking is a third mode

EXAMPLES OF IDEA FRAGMENTS

CHAPTER ONE: THRILL!

The thrill of peak experiences can be used in the workplace to produce a great performance and overcome a risk-averse culture.

Fragments: Peak performance, emotional response to the physical thrill, large-scale Navy operation, overcoming adversity, positive and negative aspects of fear

CHAPTER TWO: LIVE ACTION

Empowering the workforce is now the table stakes to play the faster ground game of business.

Fragments: Role clarity, extremely young workforce, empowerment, speed, knowledge and skill, continuous training

CHAPTER THREE: SACRIFICE

Sacrifice and pride can be leveraged to advance the business agenda, particularly on topics such as social sustainability.

Fragments: Personal stories, experience, hardship, purpose, participation

CHAPTER FOUR: FAITH AT WORK

Building a compassionate culture through chaplains or other spiritual advisors can create a better kind of business.

Fragments: Limitations, mentor, coach, spirituality, compassion, communication of processing. This is a type of inductive thinking that comes from the blend of a physical experience with mental processing. We know there is a link between body and mind; take the concept of embodied cognition. In her article "Six Views of Embodied Cognition" (*Psychonomic Bulletin and Review*, vol. 9, no. 4), Margaret Wilson, associate professor at the University of California, Santa Cruz, defines embodied cognition as "the idea that the mind must be understood in the context of its relationship to a physical body that interacts with the world." In an immersion, you physically engage your body in the experience as a way to stimulate conductive thinking. It is what sets an immersion apart from other approaches to creativity.

In a letter to his brother, the artist Vincent Van Gogh described how he got his creative ideas: through direct contact. That is to say, creativity can be found by really immersing in whatever situation you are in, without holding back. When Van Gogh died at the age of thirty-seven, he left behind a legacy of energy and emotion in the form of more than two thousand drawings and paintings. Van Gogh's efforts reveal that when he worked, he transcended boundaries and deeply focused on the moment.

In an immersion, you are engulfed in the experience. Letting go during this experience allows you to move away from your

WHAT DO YOU DO WHEN YOU RUN OUT OF IDEAS?

Sometimes a new technique can provide fresh-squeezed ideas. Forget the tried-and-true tactics you have used before, and try an immersion to stimulate conductive thinking. It will produce novel thinking patterns and challenge your assumptions.

Chapter 15 provides a list of ideas for immersions you can undertake yourself or with a team, ranging from orchid hunting to NASCAR racing. Try picking one to explore your assumptions and boundaries.

current situation to a new starting point for your imagination. To find new pieces that don't fit with what you know. To collect them. To see new clusters and combinations that are stimulated by the physical and mental combination of conductive thinking.

It is a seductive experience to be temporarily in the darker or lighter corners of an immersion, where you might not otherwise have allowed yourself to go. You find yourself truly living in the moment as the experience spontaneously enters your mind, then filtering new thoughts, and then seeing them on their way. The physical space unfolds around you in the experience and merges with your inner space as you move through the immersion. You are constantly processing new learning that is combined physically and mentally. Your sensation of time and space become newly connected as they are at the "edge of physics." A dense net forms of possible references and relationships. You must lean into the situation to maximize what you get out of it. Let go, and do your best.

CHAPTER ELEVEN

AFFECTING DECISIONS

THE DEEPER REASONS FOR OUR CHOICES

Imagine the stress as a pilot closes in on the target. His mission can only end somewhere down in the black ocean before him. The aircraft carrier appears as a rectangular box, impossibly small, moving away from him. His only comfort is the voice of the landing signal officer talking him through speed, altitude, and position. A typical airport runway is more than a mile long and pointed into the prevailing wind to bring a plane down smoothly anywhere along it. A carrier's landing area, on the other hand, is less than 150 feet from the first arresting wire to the last. Come in too high and you miss all the wires and have to take off and try again. Come in too low and you'll plow into the carrier's stern. The runway of a carrier is angled to the left of the ship's center, and because the ship is constantly moving, the runway pulls away from the pilot and to the right.

The pilot levels the wings and squares up with the carrier's stern. Now he's within a mile of the ship, and he's off his instruments, talking only to the landing signal officer. Up or down. Left or right. Slow or fast. He hits the deck hard at 150 to 170 miles per hour, then guns the engine in case he has to take off again. The pilot doesn't know he's safe until he is thrown forward in his seat, his captured plane struggling to break free of the arresting wire, like a lion caught in a net. Under his seat he can feel the hot roar of the engine.

To be successful at a task with so little margin for error, pilots face a lengthy and stressful series of qualifications, both day and night, on land and at sea. There is no time to consciously consider decisions in the last twenty seconds of the landing. Pilots have to make decisions at a precognitive, or subconscious, level of thinking. This know-how is, alas, perishable—hard earned and quickly lost. So when a carrier prepares to deploy, its air wing (which consists of several aircraft squadrons) heads back to school at an outlying landing field to practice.

As part of the training initiative, the U.S. military is working on technologies to improve pilot performance through brain sensors and intelligent computing that can adapt to what a human is thinking. To put it simply, people have more than one kind of working memory and more than one kind of attention. There are separate parts of the mind for things written, things heard, and things seen. Since 2000 the Pentagon has spearheaded augmented cognition and neurotechnology programs to build prototype cockpits that sense what is occupying a pilot's attention and adjust how information is displayed accordingly.

These technologies tap each pilot's subconscious reactions and adapt the necessary information in the cockpit. By monitoring the extent to which the different areas of the brain are taxed, the computer can adapt its display to compensate in real time. If a pilot is getting too much information via his or her headphones, send a text alert. If he or she is overloaded with words, present some of the data visually—in a chart or map. Imagine if you had the advantage of such a system at work to guide your attention and improve decisions! (I want it. Now.)

At Boeing Phantom Works, researchers are using augmented cognition technologies to design tomorrow's cockpits and pilot helmets. Boeing's prototype system uses real-time analysis to check just how overloaded a pilot's visual and verbal memories are. Then the system adjusts its interface by popping up the most important images on the screen, suggesting what targets should be hit next and, eventually, taking over for the pilot entirely if his brain becomes completely overwhelmed.

Tremendous progress is being made through these programs to improve message and information assessment and to increase pilot performance by presenting the right information at the right time based on the individual's mental processing. Some of the simulation research uses brain scan equipment like an EEG; it looks like a swim cap placed on the pilot's head to measure brain waves through the scalp and thus assess the rate at which incoming messages are processed. The technology cannot read the thoughts of the pilot, but it can monitor attention and engagement to improve pilot performance and decisions.

Only 15 percent of the decisions we make are made consciously or rationally. Certainly our conscious mind can override our subconscious impulses, but it takes a lot of mental energy to do so. The significant point here is that the military is using technology to tap into the pilots' subconscious, where 85 percent of all our decisions are processed. The commercial world can also leverage these advances in neuroscience and technology to better understand choice.

SPECTACULAR POINT

New insights using neuroscience research techniques are available to business to better understand customer preferences and decisions.

Malcom Gladwell's best-selling book *Blink: The Power of Thinking Without Thinking* (Little, Brown & Co., 2005) is about the fundamental way we think that is beyond our rational, conscious mind. The book focuses on the powerful force of the preconscious mind and how it affects our everyday decisions and behaviors, particularly in the business world. This is the same approach the military is taking to enhance pilot performance by tapping into the subconscious decisions during flight. Those instantaneous impressions and conclusions are also at work in how customers make choices.

The human mind is an incredible system whose perceptual and decision-making capabilities stem from our neurological system, which has been hardwired over billions of years of evolution to use efficient "shortcuts" to make quick decisions. Humans draw upon instinct, memory, and symbolic patterns to evaluate billions of stimuli before merely a tiny fraction of that stimulus shower enters our consciousness at any moment. Our brain automatically just filters out most of this stimulus without our even being aware of it.

As neuroscience continues to develop, business will be able to better understand preferences, purchasing decisions, and even customer aspirations, giving us much more insight than is accessible through traditional market research methods. A wide range of established neuroscience methods are already available for observing and measuring subconscious attitudes and behaviors. Using fMRI (or functional magnetic resonance imaging) and other biometric technologies, DaimlerChrysler's research center in Ulm, Germany, is studying the brains of drivers as they interact with cars. Some of that work is intended to design navigational systems for safer vehicles. Some is driven by marketing to assess the deeper motivations and preferences for specific car designs.

The new knowledge about human behavior is brought to light by neuroscience and social science and has fundamentally called into question the old models of how advertising and marketing work on the consumer's brain. Gone are the notions that consumers make decisions in a linear way and that behavior is guided by rational principles only. Instead, memories, emotions, associations, and thoughts play the overarching role in how individuals relate to and ultimately engage in choice. Brands are an efficient mental shortcut people rely on to make choices. Much of the power of a brand is implicit and subconscious, and its strength is a function of its ability to "come to mind" in appropriate circumstances, such as shopping.

Just as the Navy is embracing neuroscience to improve performance, business has the opportunity to do the same. Accessing the power of this science will open up a new level of deep insights that will allow an organization to better serve customers. Right now we are only scratching the surface of the vast customer insights that may be available beyond self-reported techniques. Take, for example, the ability to measure the effects of emotional arousal on decision making, a measurement that can be carried out quite effortlessly with portable scan technology. These research techniques are well developed and priced in line with more traditional research methods. The only barrier to their use that exists is the willingness to give it a try.

A number of leading companies are ahead of the curve in this area: DaimlerChrysler, Frito-Lay, Yahoo!, Microsoft, and Disney, to name a few. They are using these techniques for product development, advertising evaluation, packaging assessment, and retail experience measurement. Their swift-footed adoption will pay back in terms of lower commercial risks and better performance. If your business lacks an understanding of the subconscious insights that neuroscience can reveal, it may be time to start sprinting. The game's afoot!

CHAPTER TWELVE

STANDARD OF EXCELLENCE

RENEWING EXCELLENCE

"Catapult" is one of those words that causes our pores to dilate as we break out in a sweat. The catapult is a device that uses energy and gravity to propel an object through the air. In this case, the projectile being hurled is a plane. I doubt the ancient Greeks had this in mind when they originally created the *katapelte* as a weapon with which to fight against Carthage.

As the airmen in green jerseys crouched under our plane to hook it onto the launch bar of the catapult, every pixel of matter and energy in my body began to jump and dance. The launch bar holds the plane in place as the steam pressure builds up and the pilot revs the engines to full power. When the plane was rocket-ready, the sailor on deck dropped his arm, signaling to the pilot it was time to blast off. Over the roaring engines, the airman shouted those now familiar words: "Let's go, let's go, let's go!"

When the catapult is activated, the shuttle along the deck shoots rapidly forward. It drags the plane with it by the launch bar, causing the water in every cell of a passenger's body to slosh and churn. In two seconds the plane accelerates from 0 to 170 miles per hour and riders are in the "eyeballs out" position—the reverse of the landing experience. During the full eight seconds of the catapult thrust, the pressure built up in my head this time, not my chest. Acceleration and force aligned in a horizontal direction as I was propelled forward. My perception was that I was in a liquid flow. No longer able to distinguish myself physically, I was radiating with the same energy as the plane. It was like being in an altered state.

And then, as suddenly as it had begun, the pressure stopped. In an instant these sensations shifted, along with my perception. What felt like the plane stopping was actually the moment it lifted off the flight deck and broke free of the force of the catapult. It took a few minutes for me to feel like a solid again and for my cells and circuits to settle down to their quiet vibrations. I knew the surging steam from the catapult brake was billowing down the flight deck behind us as the plane ascended into the sky. It was a scene straight out of the movie *Top Gun*.

My departure from the *Stennis* was as thrilling as the arrival. The experience was completely immersive. In fact, the exhilaration I felt throughout the trip—from the landing to the liftoff and all parts in between—was a result of going through the five steps of thrill during this peak experience. Arousal by and anxiety about the risk had waxed and waned in my head even in the weeks before the trip. In the end, my excitement about learning and growing overwhelmed my fears on the day I boarded the COD heading out to the *Stennis*.

Some time later I thought about why fear didn't prevent me from taking this trip. Among the reasons, a big one was simple trust: I had put myself into the hands of the Navy because I perceived that organization as being extremely competent. I was confident in the level of excellence I would encounter.

Excellence is achieved in the military through collective action in pursuit of shared high-performance goals. The armed forces demand the kind of effort and restraint, drive and discipline that make for a great performance. Meeting these lofty goals requires the vigilant alignment of individual and group expectations, a process that at times may be difficult, as the group must find ways to deal with the circumstances that can often lead individual group members to withhold their best efforts. The Navy produces a climate in which there is pride in operating at a high level of excellence to achieve shared goals. Yet as in any group, there is a great tangle of diverse and distinct individual motives that must be taken into consideration. Not everyone is enjoying their military experience. Add to this the ever-shifting pool of young talent the military has to train in the mastery of complex skills, and it means these organizations must continuously focus on physical and mental renewal. Excellence has to constantly be reinvented.

SPECTACULAR POINT
Renewal is a key component of excellence.

As Apple CEO and innovative entrepreneur Steve Jobs has said, "Some people aren't used to an environment where excellence is expected." A common definition of excellence is the mark of achievement that significantly distinguishes work from the mainstream. Yet everyone's perspective of excellence is different, and everyone's perspective matters if a group is to unite behind collective goals.

CHAPTER 12: STANDARD OF EXCELLENCE

Society is now experiencing a shift as profound as the original Renaissance, providing the opportunity to reinvigorate excellence. In such times of renewal, new ideas spring forward. Learning what makes your company work, and what makes it valuable to world commerce, is necessary now more than ever in today's changing and confused marketplace. This will require a renewed reliance on our own expertise to define excellence—and to throw overboard the old rules, paradigms, rituals, and explanations. Renewal requires you to wake up your thinking and pioneer change, to catapult your business ahead of others. Mastery and creativity will have to be applied in order to imagine a new level of performance that goes beyond the notion of best practice. In other words, your organization must differentiate your work from the ordinary so that it bears the mark of achievement.

We must come to recognize that excellence is very hard work and that it is the key to innovation from the inside out. When we survey the corporate world, it becomes clear that rehabilitation will be required ahead. Too few companies can hold up shiny examples of their excellence. The primary barriers to this have less to do with competition and more to do with whether you can engage deeply in your own enterprise to identify the standard of excellence your business can achieve—and to prioritize the resources to get there.

Let's review some of the themes in this book that can be applied to a strategy to renew excellence:

1. Thrill: Energize your workforce around this concept. Set up one or two small teams and give them the support and the freedom to drive a project to a higher goal than the business would have set before. When the people involved develop and stretch to the limit, even for short periods of time, they will experience the thrill of personal excellence.

2. Sacrifice: Excite your company with an inspiring vision that will require a new level of commitment to achieve excellence. The sacrifice necessary to open the door to higher levels of excellence has to have a more intrinsic reward for the participants than a paycheck. The vision has to matter to the people who stand ready to commit to a larger purpose.

3. Pride: Define a remarkable goal that will motivate people to participate. Pride is produced when others can see the merit of the effort. If you have a tangible product, as Apple does, it is easier for the work to be seen. If the performance involves a service or process,

like Google search, you have to work harder to make the impact and accomplishments visible for others to appreciate.
4. Immersion: Project a culture of openness to learning and commitment in order to stimulate ongoing personal growth. An immersion provides a continual process of self-discovery, and supporting those discoveries will lead people to reach for new creative opportunities, pushing them to redefine boundaries of excellence. Create an immersive experience for top talent to attend.

High-level performers are great at generating their own best path. They carry a positive perspective, respect what works best for them, focus fully, and continue to look for ways to improve. This becomes so natural for some wildly talented people that they are able to follow their path consistently without much conscious awareness. But most people need more extrinsic motivation, like the four strategies just described, to make the major expenditure of effort and energy that excellence requires. The military leverages these motivations very well to drive such a consistently high level of performance across a wide spectrum of disciplines.

Like armed forces personnel, employees at all levels must be responsible for excellence in their own performance. Consider whether excellence is currently exhibited in your company at the rate you need to win. Is it time for you to reboot?

GIVE IT A TRY

Ask the people in your company to submit examples of excellence from their team or division. Invite them to stand up for fifteen minutes to present an idea or share work they are doing. Then decide whether excellence is being demonstrated among your workforce. If not, what can you do about it? Minimally, it is an opportunity to redefine excellence to set common goals for people to strive for. Where excellence is demonstrated, you have the basis for sustainable competitive advantage that should be nurtured and protected.

CHAPTER THIRTEEN

MILITARY MIGHT

WHY THE MILITARY IS A TALENT POOL FOR BUSINESS

I entered the Officers' Mess, and standing before me was a man wearing a T-shirt that read in large, bold letters across the chest, FUN BOSS. All that was missing was an exclamation mark. Having met the air boss and the gun boss earlier in the trip, I knew that this man's job was signaled right there on his chest. He took the time to tell me that his role was to create innovative recreation activities while at sea and on shore. The goal is to improve morale and reduce the stress of deployment through activities such as card games, movie nights, area tours, and trips. It turns out he is a civilian on board.

The fun boss and I stepped into the dining room, where already the gun boss (wearing a red T-shirt with the same bold lettering) was talking about his years on a submarine, comparing its cramped quarters to the spaciousness of the *Stennis*. As the men of fun and guns stood there side by side in their lettered T-shirts, I was struck by the juxtaposition of revival and performance. These two concepts go together like the fox-trot, where the first and third steps of the dance are more strongly accented than the second and fourth are. It is a combination of slow and quick steps to maintain equilibrium throughout the dance. In other words, you must have the ability to step to two different beats to maintain harmony. Surely this two-beat concordance is necessary to balance the on-off emotional demands of military life.

As I later reflected on that dinner I had shared with the executive officer's team, I realized that our closest connection around the table of twenty people was leadership. We are all in the people business. The scale of human energy on the *Stennis* is enormous, even for someone from a multinational corporation. Containing human energy and applying it with purpose lies at the very essence of business. The military can say the same.

Human energy is the most important resource in business today. The greater the physical, intellectual, and emotional energy a company possesses, the more competitive it will be. The number of hours in a day is fixed, but the level of energy available is not.

The maximum energy level of 100 percent is achieved when everyone in the organization is fully engaged.

SPECTACULAR POINT
Servicemen and women have the potential to be high-energy corporate athletes.

About 1.5 million American men and women, from all walks of life, wear the uniform of the armed services of the United States military and stand to defend freedom in 120 nations around the globe. Many of them are in Afghanistan and Iraq. They are serving in countries most of them had never seen before, fighting for strangers in the name of freedom. They are the heroes of our time. More than 200,000 people are discharged from the military every year and are seeking jobs in civilian life.

Potential employers should view these young men and women as a talent pool of elite athletes. They are people with the necessary mental optimism and physical stamina; they have been trained to work hard and achieve. Through their military training, they have learned:

- To be resilient and flexible in the face of nonstop stress

- To be productive and effective by managing their energy
- To balance energy between performance and revival
- To lead through any circumstance to accomplish the objective

In 1994 Lieutenant Colonel Jacquelyn "Jackie" Susan Parker became the first American woman in the Air Force to become combat qualified to fly the F-16 and be assigned to a fighter squadron. I met her quite by accident at a conference and could not resist the chance to get a pilot's perspective on the subject of this chapter. I wanted to know: What skills do pilots develop that can be leveraged in the commercial world? Her response highlighted qualities such as leadership, judgment under pressure, and strong analytic skills that allow a person to process a wide variety of information quickly in order to make sound decisions. All these are leadership skills that are relevant in the business world. Some companies have also recognized the leadership and judgment skills that Jackie mentioned. Firms like Google, Amazon, and Procter & Gamble are working with the MBA Veterans Network to identify and recruit potential candidates. The network also operates an online social site to target the far-flung MBA-credentialed veteran population.

The U.S. Department of Labor's list of the top ten reasons to hire a veteran is provided on the next four pages. Each one is a worthwhile reason to seek talent among those who have experienced this fast-forward college of another kind. My personal addition to the Department of Labor list—yet another reason former military personnel will enhance your organization's productivity—would be "Catalysts of energy." Leaders who can manage their energy more effectively are more productive in the workplace. A high-performing workplace is characterized by high-energy people pointed toward shared goals. In the same way that the moon influences the tides, people with high energy exert a magnetic pull on organizations. Great people, empowered to do great things, will pull business into an orbit of growth.

10 REASONS TO HIRE VETS

1. **Accelerated learning curve:** Veterans have the proven ability to learn new concepts. In addition, they can enter your workforce with identifiable and transferable skills, proven in real-world situations. This background can enhance your organization's productivity.
2. **Leadership:** The military trains people to lead by example as well as through direction, delegation, motivation, and inspiration. Veterans understand the practical ways to manage behaviors for results, even in the most trying circumstances. They also know the dynamics of leadership as part of both hierarchical and peer structures.
3. **Teamwork:** Veterans understand how genuine teamwork grows out of a responsibility to one's colleagues. Military duties involve a blend of individual and group productivity. They also necessitate a perception of how groups of all sizes relate to each other and an overarching objective.

4. **Diversity and inclusion in action:** Veterans have learned to work side by side with individuals regardless of diverse race, gender, geographic origin, ethnic background, religion, and economic status as well as mental, physical, and attitudinal capabilities. They have the sensitivity to cooperate with many different types of individuals.
5. **Efficient performance under pressure:** Veterans understand the rigors of tight schedules and limited resources. They have developed the capacity to know how to accomplish priorities on time, in spite of tremendous stress. They know the critical importance of staying with a task until it is done right.
6. **Respect for procedures:** Veterans have gained a unique perspective on the value of accountability. They can grasp their place within an organizational framework, becoming responsible for subordinates' actions to higher supervisory levels. They know how policies and procedures enable an organization to exist.

7. **Technology and globalization:** Because of their experiences in the service, veterans are usually aware of international and technical trends pertinent to business and industry. They can bring the kind of global outlook and technological savvy that all enterprises of any size need to succeed.
8. **Integrity:** Veterans know what it means to do "an honest day's work." Prospective employers can take advantage of a track record of integrity, often including security clearances. This integrity translates into qualities of sincerity and trustworthiness.
9. **Conscious of health and safety standards:** Thanks to extensive training, veterans are aware of health and safety protocols both for themselves and the welfare of others. Individually, they represent a drug-free workforce that is cognizant of maintaining personal health and fitness. On a company level, their awareness and conscientiousness translate into protection of employees, property, and materials.

10. **Triumph over adversity:** In addition to dealing positively with the typical issues of personal maturity, veterans have frequently triumphed over great adversity. They likely have proven their mettle in mission-critical situations demanding endurance, stamina, and flexibility. They may have overcome personal disabilities through strength and determination.

Source: U.S. Department of Labor's Hire Vets First initiative (www.hirevetsfirst.dol.gov)

AIRCRAFT PARKED ON THE DECK
OF THE USS *STENNIS*.

CHAPTER FOURTEEN

TOP TEN TAKEAWAYS

A CALL TO ACTION FOR THE READER

1. *Start* now to harness the excitement of "thrill" in order to fulfill company goals and personal dreams and to leverage top talent in your organization.
2. *Follow* the seven steps in chapter 2 to empower your workforce to "move the organization out of the way" in order to increase operating speed.
3. *Challenge* whether the higher purpose of your organization motivates people enough to sacrifice what is needed to reach an extraordinary goal.
4. *Leverage* compassion to build a culturally savvy organization capable of empathizing with diverse customers and partners for competitive advantage.

5. *Create* an anticipation barometer to measure whether your business adequately gauges emerging opportunities and risks. Identify who leads this visionary work and how it is applied internally to produce the nimbleness necessary to flex the corporate muscles at just the right time.
6. *Champion* badges of purpose that resurrect the value of corporations to society. Invest in the issues to which corporations are well poised to contribute, in order to earn the loyalty of employees and customers alike.
7. *Contract* with a game developer such as Autodesk or Schell Games to build an interactive strategy game for your company. Completely rethink the current lenses and templates you use for strategy today, and enhance performance by creating an interactive platform to link the present and the future.
8. *Use* the structure of an immersion to generate fresh insights and to innovate in extraordinary ways. Read chapter 15 for suggested immersions, or create others with your team. If you are looking for resources, IDEO is an organization that understands the power of an immersive experience to stimulate innovation.

9. *Evaluate* the core business capabilities, and identify which one or two you will accelerate to a new standard of excellence in the industry. Define what it will take to do it, and get started.
10. *Connect* with a military recruiting firm such as Orion International or Lucas Group. Identify open positions for veteran recruiting to energize your workforce.

We keep moving forward, opening new doors, and doing new things, because we are curious—and curiosity keeps leading us down new paths.

—Walt Disney

CHAPTER FIFTEEN

ARE YOU READY TO TAKE AN IMMERSION?

Immersing myself in the life an aircraft carrier provided me with spectacular moments that forever changed my perspective on business and life. You can find spectacular moments in your own life and the life of your organization that will reawaken the spirit of adventure and discovery. Spectacular experiences will sandblast the ordinary from your operations and unleash the potential energy that will propel your people to unlimited commitment and success. Some of the immersive experiences you might want to explore are described on the next few pages.

ORCHID HUNTING

What? Yes, that's right: orchid hunting. Would it surprise you to know that the international orchid business brings in $10 billion annually? Orchids are the most highly evolved flowering plants on Earth. Even more interesting is the fact that they are ancient plants that have outlived the dinosaurs. You can hunt orchids from Cuba to Malaysia to New Jersey. Summertime field trips are available in Manitoba, Canada, where participants venture through the wetlands to find fringed orchids.

Perhaps you should start by reading *The Orchid Thief* by Susan Orlean. The book captures the intrigue and politics of the orchid business. Orchid hunting is an interesting intersection among the worlds of nature, gardening, and commerce. Science has labeled ideas that are based on solutions created by Mother Nature as "biomimicry." Velcro, for example, was an idea that came from a walk in the woods through burrs. Imagine the ideas that await you as you step into wetlands and woods to commune with nature as you search for orchids.

GLASSBLOWING

Glassblowing is truly a process. Your skill builds with practice, however, in as little as one week. The work is done in pairs, and the steps are synchronized moves as you twirl the molten glass that has been gathered from a furnace at 2200 degrees Fahrenheit. Remarkably, after just one day, the beginner can make a basic bowl or vase. Eventually the work evolves to adding color to the glass, and opportunities for creativity increase as the basics are mastered. The Pittsburgh Glass Center is one example of a facility that offers full-day or weeklong classes for the novice. Even award-winning glass artists, such as Brayton Furlong in Northern California (BraytonFurlong.com), will arrange for private instruction.

Glassblowing combines process thinking and mechanics to achieve creativity. The focus is on efficiency in the work and how decisions during action produce something new. It is a world of new language and sensations, and it is amazing to see how the odd wooden tools of the glassblower produce imaginative products from sand, water, and heat. If you develop good ideas while taking a shower or on a long drive, the glassblowing experience is sure to suit you; it is possible to tap more of those subconscious thoughts as you become immersed in the world of artisans and craftsmen. Themes of pride and accomplishment also will be revealed in this experience.

TAKE A "VOCATION VACATION"

Vocation Vacations is a company that is enriching people's lives by allowing them to test-drive a career. While taking a vacation of two to three days, you can immerse yourself in a completely new discipline through one of 125 career choices, such as: Be a Farmer, Be a Broadway Director, Be an Architect, or Be a Nonprofit Director.

You may or may not be able to convince your employer to foot the bill for this experience, which usually has a price tag of under $1,000. Try defining it as an immersion rather than a vacation when you discuss it with your boss!

What you get out of the experience will obviously depend on the type of career experience you choose. Think about how the theme may connect you to your customers or offer strategic business potential. If you work for Kraft Foods, for example, the Be a Chef experience may not open your eyes to new possibilities as much as the Be a Restaurant Critic or Be a Sommelier experience. Sink your teeth into something new.

DEEP FLIGHT SCHOOL

The Deep Flight Underwater Flight School operates out of Monterey, California, at the National Marine Sanctuary. It is a once-in-a-lifetime opportunity to explore the ocean by "flying" underwater in a state-of-the-art underwater Super Falcon. There are several options to experience deep-sea flight at the school: one sixty-minute dive for $2,500; two dives and training to fly the plane yourself for $5,000; or a three-day training and pilot licensing course for $15,000.

Our oceans contain 99 percent of the living space on the planet, yet humans have explored less than 10 percent of them. The excitement of exploration awaits you as you enter the mysterious underwater world of the sea on a Deep Flight excursion. The threatened state of our oceans and the sustainability of the planet are significant themes to be explored as part of the experience. Excellence through technology and discovery also will be a major theme of this immersion.

NASCAR WEEKEND

The world of NASCAR is an exciting social extravaganza. Its far-reaching popularity has made it the second-most popular pro sport in this country, and it is broadcast in more than 150 other countries. The sport boasts a fan base of about 75 million, and they are some of the most devoted sports fans in the world. Each race is an awe-inspiring flurry of sound, color, and emotion. Prior to the start of the race, there is a stirring show of patriotism that includes the national anthem, often accompanied by a ceremonial military aircraft flyby. On the ground, the drivers fire up their finely tuned machines after being given the command, "Drivers, start your engines!"

Intense competition surrounded by devoted fans—it's a hyper-lens for business. What does it take to build such devoted fans for your product or service? The NASCAR experience is a grassroots immersion in mass-market fans, product sponsorships, and endorsements. Attending a NASCAR event gets you up close and personal with more than 120,000 mass-market customers who are motivated by the sense of belonging and connection they experience at these supersized events. You will also have the opportunity to witness thrill and its effects. It's sure to have an impact on you, too, stimulating the rush of dopamine needed to create new ideas.

A DAY TO YOURSELF

If you are like most people, it has been a long time since you have been alone with your thoughts for an entire day. This immersion is a chance to unclog your brain to refresh and recalibrate yourself. When the mind is spinning with day-to-day demands and distractions, it is hard to get new ideas to flow. To stimulate the conductive thinking offered by an immersion, you will need to choose a physical activity to undertake for the day. Physically engaging your body in the experience is a way to help unlock your thoughts.

Activities such as biking, hiking, painting, skating, gardening, or swimming will stimulate juicy subconscious thoughts. The physical activity allows these circulating thoughts to break into your consciousness, where they can be assembled into new patterns and ideas. Spend the day in a place that you find inspiring, and enjoy yourself.

SHARE YOUR IMMERSION

Conductive thinking is an area that business has not paid attention to for innovation and inspiration. We are interested in tracking the adventures that readers undertake and the stories they have to tell about their quest to stimulate ideas by experiencing new worlds.

Stories and photos can be posted at http://www.facebook.com/donna.sturgess.

CHAPTER SIXTEEN

USING THE IMMERSION EXPERIENCE

Once you have experienced the power of an immersion, consider taking the following steps toward inspiring an exceptional workforce and rebooting the thrill of overwhelming success. Feel free to use these exercises as an individual or in a group setting. As you take off to new levels of inspiration, you will feel the power—eyeballs out!

SENSING THE SPECTACULAR

Take a moment to consider your own spectacular moments. What experience took your breath away? When did you last feel your pulse racing and your head spinning? What visions came to you in that moment of ecstatic inspiration? How did your perspective change? Toward your business? Toward your personal life?

We have all had spectacular moments, though we may not have experienced them fully. Do you recall a time when you had the opportunity for a spectacular experience but held back? Why did you hold back? Fear? Anxiety? Unwillingness to step into a new realm of experience?

Now go back to that moment. In your mind, take the chance to immerse yourself in the memory of the experience. How does that feel? Do any insights come to you?

Spectacular moments allow us to tap into our well of inspiration and prepare us for the inspiration that surely lies ahead.

REALIZE YOUR DREAMS

You can use the energy from immersive experiences to help you and others fulfill company goals and realize personal dreams. What are your company goals? Do you feel inspired to achieve these goals or is there something missing? If you don't feel the inspiration for your goals, open up to the possibility of creating new goals. What would these new goals be? Do they spring from your spectacular moments?

Now shift focus to your personal dreams. Can you visualize these dreams? How do your personal dreams intertwine with your company goals? Will fulfilling your dreams lead to more immersive experiences?

Let others know that fulfilling company goals should help them realize their personal dreams. See what dreams or goals excite your top talent and share with them the spectacular moment of realizing those goals.

EMBRACE RISK

When we allow ourselves to experience spectacular moments, we learn to embrace the risk of the unknown. What has been the biggest risk you have taken in your business? In your personal life?

How did you feel when confronted with that risk? What made you decide to take the risk? When did you understand the result of taking that risk? What were the benefits? What were the costs?

Are you more willing to take risks today than you've been in the past? If not, why not?

Make a list of the risks you face at this moment in your life. Consider your options, including whether or not the risks offer the opportunity for a spectacular moment. Tap into your reservoir of confidence as you visualize what will happen if you make the plunge. Remember, the thrill of your peak experiences will help you become less risk averse.

INCREASE YOUR SPEED

The pace of business increases hourly, as worldwide integration of markets and production creates an ever-faster business cycle. Our experiences change the way we look at time, as inspiration brings instantaneous action. What happens to time during a spectacular moment? Does every insight bring astounding possibilities? Do you have the power to act faster than anyone else?

Train yourself to shift into high gear by tapping the energy of your spectacular moments. Make each spectacular moment a moment of inspiration and accomplishment.

Consider the speed with which your organization responds to change. How can you translate the immediacy of a spectacular moment to your entire workforce? Work with key individuals to rely on their strongest inspirations as they tackle the toughest business challenges. Then get out of their way.

DEVELOP PRIDE

By inspiring self-awareness, spectacular moments strengthen feelings of self-worth. With rejuvenated energy and a firm grounding in your own abilities, you develop a sense of pride that extends from yourself to the world around you. What are you most proud of in your business life? In your personal life? Has that pride come from a spectacular moment?

A sense of pride allows you to make the sacrifices you need to achieve an extraordinary outcome. What sacrifices have you made to achieve your goals? Are you willing to make sacrifices for goals that stretch beyond your business agenda?

Explore the higher goals of your workforce. Energy sustainability? Helping feed local families? Improving the health of the community? Make a list of activities that your organization can do together, accepting the sacrifices you need to make to work toward those high goals.

USE COMPASSION

A spectacular moment brings with it feelings of openness. With the revelation of the immersive experience comes a new perspective on those around us. How did an immersive experience change your attitude toward those closest to you? Did that attitude extend to those with whom you work?

Compassion brings you closer to others. As you come to understand the concerns of others, you learn to share in their successes as well as their setbacks. List those people for whom you have developed compassion. Now, think about others in your organization.

Consider yourself and your workforce. Do you have a culture of compassion? Do your workers support one another? Do they have compassion for clients and customers?

Think about working with a spiritual advisor to help develop a culture of compassion. Engaging the soul will deepen the impact of a spectacular moment.

ANTICIPATE TO OVERCOME

Anticipation requires strong perceptual skills. Only people who have a high-definition sensitivity to changing patterns in the operating environment and the leadership skills to act upon the emerging information are able to truly anticipate the future. Do you recall a time when you were surprised by a competitor's move? What would you have done to anticipate that move?

Developing a competency in anticipation requires finding people who are capable of the task. You need individuals who have a "touch" for the environment or situation, a sensitivity to future trends, and strong intuitive skills. You may have anticipation skills or you may already know people in your organization who have these skills. Find these people, bring them together, and form a team of visionaries. Be honest with yourself. Are you a visionary who can lead this team, or should you play the role of facilitator, interpreting the trend spotting of others?

Identify a leader for this team. Working with the team, create an anticipation barometer to measure whether or not your business adequately gauges future opportunities and risks. Develop an internal process that will allow you to anticipate, act, and beat the competition.

EMOTIONAL MEDICINE

Laughter serves as emotional medicine to cut down on anxiety and relieve stress. People who are able to find humor in even the toughest situations can help others turn stress into a positive—a catalyst for hard work, commitment, and timely execution.

How do you use laughter to forge the bonds between people?

Do you yourself discourage humor, or do you view it as positive, work-enhancing behavior? Who in your organization can bring laughter and success to a team? Can you remember any instances in which humor helped you get the job done?

Consider a situation that is causing you stress. Now, take the time to consciously change your perspective. Go beyond your comfort zone. Find the humor in your situation and share a laugh with someone on your team. A small moment of pleasure can disrupt a great deal of stress. The emotional medicine of laughter can clarify your thinking and bring your team together.

LEVERAGING NEUROSCIENCE

Science has expanded our ability to understand the motivations and behaviors of those around us. Neuroscience research techniques bring us new insights into the activity of our own brain and allow us to better understand our customers.

How do your customers perceive your product and/or service? How do they make their purchasing decisions? What deep insights do you have into customer motivations?

Have you incorporated insights from the nonconscious into your own sales and marketing plans? Dig deep. Go beyond rational motivations and consider the emotional aspects of the purchasing decision. Start viewing your customers as complex personalities rather than as rational decision makers. They have many motivations that you cannot access by asking direct questions and receiving direct answers. And examine your own decision-making processes as well.

MAKE IT A GAME

Sometimes it's healthy to view business, and life, as a game. It's a tough game, for sure. Jobs and income depend on who wins or loses the business game, but it is a game nonetheless. And sometimes stepping back and considering business from a more dispassionate perspective can help you rethink your strategy and get more competitive.

What game do you enjoy? Why do you enjoy it? What does the game provide you in terms of insight into others? Into yourself?

Get together with some people from your organization who are familiar with online strategy games. Talk with them about designing an interactive strategy game for your company. List three key elements that the game will have.

Consider producing an interactive game to manage your

business strategy. There are many resources available to create a proprietary game to step-change the way you manage your business strategy. Taking a fresh, new competitive attitude toward your company's core decision-making process could be a game changer.

SEEK OUT IMMERSION EXPERIENCES

Successfully operating a business requires continuous innovation inspired by fresh insights. Immersion experiences can bring those insights in extraordinary ways. An immersion experience brings out fragments of new ideas from new sights, sounds, smells, tastes, and textures that can trigger deep emotional responses and amazing revelations.

Describe your most recent immersion experience. How did it differ from the experience of your daily life? What insights came to you during the experience?

Now get together with your team or a select group of coworkers. Share with one another your most powerful immersive experiences and the new ideas that came from them. Can you apply any of these ideas to your current organization? How can you recreate these immersion experiences to bring further insights? Plan an activity that will plunge your group into an unfamiliar circumstance and be prepared for immersion illumination.

DEMAND EXCELLENCE

Organizations can flourish only if they are performing to the peak of their abilities. Excellence in every aspect of a business is an absolute necessity in today's intensely competitive market. You can't rely on past definitions of excellence. What was excellent yesterday is probably not even acceptable today.

Take an inventory of the old rules, paradigms, and explanations that you once used to measure excellence. Now, tear up the list. What does excellence mean in today's market? What benchmarks can you use to measure excellence? How do you differentiate yourself from others and truly achieve excellence?

Ask each member of your organization to identify one or two of their core business capabilities that they can elevate to a new standard of excellence. Help them define what it will take to get that started, provide the necessary resources, and watch your organization stretch beyond best practices to a new level of performance.

CONNECT TO THE WORLD

Employees and customers are no longer satisfied with isolated organizations. To earn loyalty, organizations must prove their value to society in general. Investment in the most pressing societal issues inspires loyalty and projects a positive image to the world.

Determine what social goals the individuals in your organization want to achieve. Better schools? Healthier lifestyles? Stronger families? Make a list of the organizations that are working to achieve those social goals. Let the individuals with common interests come together as a team and reach out into the community. As they do, create badges to acknowledge participation in different projects. These badges will let the world know about the dedication and sacrifices of each individual and will increase your organization's visibility within the community. As you connect with the world, the world will empower your organization.

CONDUCIVE THINKING

Immersion enables you to open up channels in your mind that are normally closed, or at least separated. In an immersion experience, you can feel the interconnection between your body and your mind, your conscious self and your unconscious self, rational thought and a dreamlike state. Have you ever made a business decision based on an insight that came to you after a long walk? This is just an indication of how an immersion experience can affect your entire thought process.

Approach your next challenge as an adventurer, not a planner. Break through the superficial issues and experience the heart of the matter. Get up from your desk and explore a new environment as you seek your answers. Are you able to feel the energy of your body and your mind coming together? Are there any other individuals in your organization who can join you in an excursion to reach a state of conductive thinking? Conductive thinking can shake up the ideas of an entire team.

As you journey to your breakthrough insight, don't be afraid of the darkness, of wondering. Your body and your mind will recombine fragments of ideas and inspirations to form new, entirely novel concepts. Open yourself up to the new extreme focus of your mental and physical energy. You will see and understand your world in a whole new way.

REVIEW AND REJUVENATE

The mind has the ultimate control over behavior and performance. In order to operate at the highest levels, the human mind must generate feelings of accomplishment and self-confidence. It does not take much to generate the necessary brain activity. A simple compliment has a strong empowering effect.

Determine how you acknowledge those around you. Do you interact with others about their performance outside of designated review periods? Do you only comment on poor execution? When was the last time you made a positive comment about someone's performance on a particular assignment? When was the last time you received a positive comment from those around you?

Open yourself up to the power of publicly recognizing competence. Even the smallest comment, if sincerely given, can motivate individuals to perform at their best.

EXPAND YOUR TEAM

As you expand your workforce, take the opportunity to reach out and discover new talent. Don't limit yourself to considering individuals with only one profile. Consider veterans, for example.

Those who have succeeded in the military have the ability to energize your organization with experience and skills honed in tough conditions.

Reach out to military recruiting firms and to other organizations that can introduce you to talented workers from all walks of life. Diversity equals energy in the workforce. A diverse organization can operate more efficiently and relate much more effectively to the increasing diversity of the marketplace.

SPECIAL THANKS

My *Stennis* trip was greatly enhanced by the following fellow adventurers:

- Phillip Barlag
- Rob Conway
- Bob Grimaila
- Jeanne Mason
- Marc Mathieu
- Jeffrey Merrihue
- Stu Pann
- Carole Seymour
- Mark Toon
- Peter Vaughn
- David Wilke

A very special thank-you goes to the U.S. Navy, and specifically to Chief Steven Harbour and Lieutenant Commander Cindy Fields for coordinating and supporting our outstanding trip.

I also want to acknowledge the team at Greenleaf who made the development of the book a simple and enjoyable process. My editor, Steve Kettmann, a former staff reporter for *New York Newsday* and the *San Francisco Chronicle,* was an enthusiast throughout the process of my telling this unusual story. His own outstanding work has included *Fish Where the Fish Are,* cowritten with Peter Arnell, and *Letter to a New President,* cowritten with the late Senator Robert Byrd.